BIBLE STUDY SERIES

HEBREWS

THE SUPREMACY OF CHRIST

DR. DAVID JEREMIAH

Prepared by Peachtree Publishing Services

Thomas Nelson
Since 1798

HEBREWS
JEREMIAH BIBLE STUDY SERIES

© 2021 by Dr. David Jeremiah

All rights reserved. No portion of this book may be reproduced, stored in a retrieval system, or transmitted in any form or by any means—electronic, mechanical, photocopy, recording, scanning, or other—except for brief quotations in critical reviews or articles, without the prior written permission of the publisher.

Published in Nashville, Tennessee, by Thomas Nelson. Thomas Nelson is a registered trademark of HarperCollins Christian Publishing, Inc.

Produced with assistance of Peachtree Publishing Service (www.PeachtreePublishingServices.com). Project staff include Christopher D. Hudson, Randy Southern, and Peter Blankenship.

All Scripture quotations are taken from The Holy Bible, New King James Version. Copyright © 1979, 1980, 1982 by Thomas Nelson. All rights reserved.

Thomas Nelson titles may be purchased in bulk for educational, business, fundraising, or sales promotional use. For information, please e-mail SpecialMarkets@ThomasNelson.com.

ISBN 978-0-310-09178-3 (softcover)
ISBN 978-0-310-09179-0 (ebook)

First Printing April 2021 / Printed in the United States of America

CONTENTS

Introduction to the Letter to the Hebrews v

Lesson 1   The Superiority of Christ (*Hebrews 1:1–14*) 1
Lesson 2   When God Became Man (*Hebrews 2:1–18*) 13
Lesson 3   A Soft Heart Toward God (*Hebrews 3:1–19*) 25
Lesson 4   Jesus Is All You Need (*Hebrews 4:1–5:14*) 37
Lesson 5   The Anchor of Hope (*Hebrews 6:1–20*) 49
Lesson 6   King and High Priest (*Hebrews 7:1–28*) 61
Lesson 7   A New Covenant (*Hebrews 8:1–9:10*) 73
Lesson 8   The Great Mediator (*Hebrews 9:11–28*) 85
Lesson 9   Faith, Hope, and Love (*Hebrews 10:1–39*) 97
Lesson 10 The Power of Faith (*Hebrews 11:1–40*) 109
Lesson 11 Running with Endurance (*Hebrews 12:1–29*) 121
Lesson 12 The Superior Life in Christ (*Hebrews 13:1–25*) 133

Leader's Guide 145
About Dr. David Jeremiah and Turning Point 150
Stay Connected to Dr. David Jeremiah 151

INTRODUCTION TO
The Letter to the Hebrews

"Let us hold fast the confession of our hope without wavering, for He who promised is faithful" (Hebrews 10:23). Jewish Christians in the first century were facing a dilemma. They had accepted Jesus as their promised Messiah, but now they were being challenged by fellow Jews who saw Jesus as a heretic or an imposter. They accused these Jewish Christians of abandoning their heritage, betraying their values, and cutting themselves off from God's people. Some of the Jewish believers were bending under the pressure. They were wondering if they had made the right choice . . . and whether it made sense to return to life under the Old Covenant. The author of Hebrews saw the danger. So he crafted this letter to them, drawing on his expansive knowledge of the Old Testament to reveal how Jesus is superior to *anything* the old law had to offer. Jesus is higher than the angels, better than any human, and their great high priest. Furthermore, Jesus accomplished what the Old Covenant could not by offering Himself as the one, true, and only perfect sacrifice that could actually atone for the sins of His people.

AUTHOR AND DATE

The author of Hebrews is unknown, and his identity has proved to be one of the enduring mysteries of the Bible. The earliest surviving copies of the New Testament grouped the letter with Paul's epistles, but early church fathers such as Irenaeus, Hippolytus, Clement, and Origen all expressed doubts. Tertullian, writing in the third century, claimed it was written by Barnabas, while Origen believed it was written by a close follower of Paul.

One theory embraced by a number of scholars is that a man named Apollos was the author. He was a Jew and would have been well educated in the Old Testament teachings and Jewish philosophy found throughout the book. He was also an associate of Timothy, who is mentioned by name in the closing. If this identity is correct, Apollos could have written the letter from Ephesus, c. AD 52–54. Regardless, most scholars believe the letter was penned before AD 70, as the author makes no mention of the destruction of the Temple in Jerusalem that occurred at that date.

Background and Setting

As with the author and date, the exact audience for the letter is also unknown. However, it can be assumed they were a group of Jewish Christians located somewhere in the Mediterranean world (possibly in Rome). The author assumes his readers are knowledgeable of the Old Testament and draws on many examples from that text to make his points. He alludes to the fact they are facing persecution for their beliefs and are feeling the pressure to return to their former way of life. The Jews viewed Jesus as a heretic, and those who followed Him were seen as traitors to their people. So these Hebrew Christians were likely facing estrangement from family, friends, and the customs of Israel because of their decision to follow Christ.

Key Themes

Several key themes are prominent in the letter to the Hebrews. The first is that *believers must recognize Jesus is better than anything that came before*. The Jewish people held their patriarchs, their prophets, their kings, and other heroes of their faith in high esteem. It was almost inconceivable that anything could be *better* than these men and women of the past whom God had raised up to accomplish such great things for His people. But this is exactly what the author of Hebrews is saying in making his case for the superiority of Christ. Jesus is superior to any person who has gone before—and even superior to angels (see 1:4–2:18, 3:1–4:13).

A second theme is that *believers must recognize Jesus as their great high priest*. The priests in the Old Testament served as intermediaries between God and His people. They represented God to the people by teaching them His holy laws. They represented the people to God by offering an unending cycle of sacrifices to atone for their sins. But when Jesus came, He instituted a completely new system, with Himself as the high priest. He fulfilled the role of the mediator by teaching God's holy laws to the people and atoning for the people's sins through His own perfect sacrifice on the cross. He is thus superior to the old system (see 4:14–7:28).

A third theme is that *believers must recognize Jesus as the all-atoning sacrifice for sin*. The Old Covenant required a sacrifice of blood to be made to atone for sin. But these animal sacrifices could not *permanently* atone for sin, so priests engaged in a constant cycle of offering them again and again. Jesus broke this cycle when He came to earth, "for by one offering He has perfected forever those who are being sanctified" (10:14). Christ thus functions under the New Covenant as *both* our high priest and as the sacrifice for sin (see 8:1–10:14).

A final theme is that *believers must persevere in their walk with Jesus*. The author, having established why it makes sense to trust in Christ, ends the letter by urging believers to apply those principles and stand strong in the face of the persecution they are facing. This would have included ostracism from society, severed relationships, and actual threats to their wellbeing. The writer draws on the examples of "heroes of the faith" who have gone before them to call out the rich benefits of trusting completely in Christ. Furthermore, their perseverance in spite of trials will serve as a powerful witness to the world (see 11:1–12:29).

Key Applications

The letter to the Hebrews reveals that following Jesus is better than following anything else that the world offers. When trials come our way, we may be tempted to doubt God's faithfulness and fall into old patterns of living. For a season, those old ways may seem to pay dividends—but in reality they are merely "passing pleasures of sin" (11:25). True and abundant life only comes by walking in step with Christ, abiding under his superior New Covenant, and persevering in spite of the trials. As we do this, like the "heroes of the faith" that have gone before us, we will enter into God's promised rest and be rewarded with eternal life.

LESSON *one*

THE SUPERIORITY OF CHRIST

Hebrews 1:1–14

Getting Started

What immediately comes to mind when you think about angels?

LETTER TO THE HEBREWS

Setting the Stage

The book of Acts tells us that many Jewish people came to faith in Christ during the early days of the church. They saw Jesus as their long-awaited Messiah who had come into the world in fulfillment of countless prophecies in the Old Testament. But the years had now passed, and the excitement was beginning to wear a bit thin. Many Jewish Christians, having been accused by their fellow Jews of abandoning their heritage, were feeling the pressure to conform and return to their old ways of life. They were wondering if following Jesus was really worth it.

This attitude troubled the author of Hebrews. It is likely that he had followed a similar path. He had accepted Jesus as the Messiah and endured the same pressures to compromise, conform, and convert back to old ways of life. But somewhere along the way, he had discovered that following Christ *really was worth it*. As he looked over the pages of Hebrew Scripture that were so familiar, he could see how the arrival of Jesus had ushered in an entirely new way for humans to relate to God that was superior to everything that had come before it.

The author begins by pointing out the superiority of the Son over the prophets of the past. But his pen doesn't linger there long, for he knows that in Jewish thought, *angels* represent the highest power next to God Himself. In truth, we find angels taking the lead role throughout the Bible when it comes to enacting God's plans. They spoke on God's behalf, delivered His messages to the nations, executed His divine orders, and protected faithful followers of God. In Jesus' life alone, we find them announcing His birth, warning His parents to flee to Egypt, ministering to Christ in the desert, rolling the stone away from the tomb, and announcing His resurrection.

The Jewish people thus held angels in high regard. One sect of Judaism, established at Qumran, taught that the archangel Michael's authority was equal to or even surpassed the authority of the Messiah. So the writer of Hebrews needed to begin there—by convincing his Jewish readers that Jesus was superior to even the most powerful of angels.

Exploring the Text

God's Supreme Revelation (Hebrews 1:1–4)

> [1] God, who at various times and in various ways spoke in time past to the fathers by the prophets, [2] has in these last days spoken to us by His Son, whom He has appointed heir of all things, through whom also He made the worlds; [3] who being the brightness of His glory and the express image of His person, and upholding all things by the word of His power, when He had by Himself purged our sins, sat down at the right hand of the Majesty on high, [4] having become so much better than the angels, as He has by inheritance obtained a more excellent name than they.

1. The Old Testament reveals that God spoke "at various times and in various ways" to His people through the prophets. These prophets spoke God's words sporadically over a great period of time. What does the author of Hebrew say has now changed in the way God speaks to His people? Why is this superior to the prophets (see verses 1–3)?

2. Jesus is stated as being "better than the angels" and having "a more excellent name." In the Bible, two prominent angels that appear are Michael and Gabriel. The name *Michael* means "who is like God," while the name *Gabriel* means "man of God." Why is Jesus' name—referring here to the title "Son"—better than that of the angels (see verse 4)?

The Son Exalted Above Angels (Hebrews 1:5–7)

⁵ For to which of the angels did He ever say:

> "You are My Son,
> Today I have begotten You"?

And again:

> "I will be to Him a Father,
> And He shall be to Me a Son"?

⁶ But when He again brings the firstborn into the world, He says:

> "Let all the angels of God worship Him."

⁷ And of the angels He says:

> "Who makes His angels spirits
> And His ministers a flame of fire."

3. The author begins to make his case about Christ in verse 5 by citing Psalm 2:7 ("You are My Son, today I have begotten You") and 2 Samuel 7:14 ("I will be his Father, and he shall be My son"). What point is he making here as it relates to Jesus' unique relationship with God? How does this make Jesus greater than the angels?

_____
_____
_____
_____
_____
_____

4. Jesus is referred to as "the firstborn" in verse 6. In both Roman and Jewish culture, this was a son who had the right of his father's inheritance. This is the only place in the letter where the author gives Jesus this designation, though elsewhere he is called God's "heir" (1:2; see also 1:4). How does this distinction of "firstborn" and "heir" set Jesus apart from the angels?

_____
_____
_____
_____
_____
_____

The Anointed One (Hebrews 1:8–11)

⁸ But to the Son He says:

> "Your throne, O God, is forever and ever;
> A scepter of righteousness is the scepter of Your kingdom.

> ⁹ You have loved righteousness and hated lawlessness;
> Therefore God, Your God, has anointed You
> With the oil of gladness more than Your companions."

¹⁰ And:

> "You, Lord, in the beginning laid the foundation of the earth,
> And the heavens are the work of Your hands.
> ¹¹ They will perish, but You remain;
> And they will all grow old like a garment . . .

---

5. The passage cited in verses 8–9 is from Psalm 45:6–7, which is a wedding song that celebrates the marriage of a king. The psalm was widely understood to look forward to the coming of the Messiah, the great future King, into the world. How does the author of Hebrews relate these lines to Jesus? How is Christ superior to all earthly kings?

6. The passage cited in verses 10–11 is from Psalm 102:25–26, which is a prayer from an afflicted person who contrasts his situation with the eternal power of the Creator. What is the author saying about Jesus by citing this passage from the Old Testament?

Seated at the Right Hand of God (Hebrews 1:12–14)

¹² Like a cloak You will fold them up,
And they will be changed.
But You are the same,
And Your years will not fail."

¹³ But to which of the angels has He ever said:

"Sit at My right hand,
Till I make Your enemies Your footstool"?

¹⁴ Are they not all ministering spirits sent forth to minister for those who will inherit salvation?

7. The passage quoted in verse 12 is from Psalm 102:25–26. All of creation will ultimately perish and be "folded up" like a worn-out cloak. But what does the author of Hebrews say about Jesus? How does this show that Jesus is equal to God?

_____
_____
_____
_____
_____
_____
_____

8. The final passage quoted in verses 13–14 is from Psalm 110:1, which reads, "The Lord said to my Lord, 'Sit at My right hand, till I make Your enemies Your footstool.'" Once again, this was widely understood to be God speaking to the Messiah. How does the writer's use of this passage help to support his point that Jesus is superior to angels?

Reviewing the Story

The author of Hebrews begins by announcing that we are in a new age. In the past, God spoke through the prophets, but today He speaks directly through the Son. The author then draws on several passages from the Old Testament to make the point that Jesus is superior to angels. Jesus' name is superior because it identifies Him as the heir of God. His glory is superior because angels worship Him. His infinite nature is superior to the angels' finite nature. And his position at God's right hand is superior to the angels' position of bowed reverence.

9. How does the writer of Hebrews summarize the things that make Jesus "so much better than the angels" (see Hebrews 1:2–4)?

10. How did Jesus' birth establish His superiority over the angels (see Hebrews 1:6)?

11. Why does Jesus' role in creation make Him superior to the angels (see Hebrews 1:10–11)?

12. What honor has God given Jesus that establishes His superiority (see Hebrews 1:13)?

Applying the Message

13. In the opening of this letter, we read that God now speaks to us through Christ. What does this mean? What are some of the ways that you have experienced God speaking to you?

14. What is the danger in giving *anything* a greater place than Christ? What happens when we give angels—or anything else—the glory that Jesus alone deserves?

Reflecting on the Meaning

The letter of Hebrews begins by stressing the superiority of Jesus to the angels. We read that Christ is "so much better than the angels" and has "a more excellent name than they" (1:4). The point being made is that Jesus alone is worthy of our praise—not angels. Yet this does not diminish the important ministry of God's angels.

The role of angels is often misunderstood today, but the Bible identifies four key roles they fulfill. *First, angels serve as God's messengers.* Messenger angels spoke to patriarchs such as Abraham and Jacob. They spoke to prophets like Daniel and priests like Zacharias. They also relayed God's messages to "regular" people, including Elizabeth, Mary, and Joseph. They delivered life-changing messages from God Himself.

Second, angels serve as ministers. Ministering angels appeared to apostles such as Peter and Paul. They cared for little children. They tended to the needs of Christ in the wilderness and in the Garden of Gethsemane. They concerned themselves with the needs of the believers. They are instruments of God's care and love.

Third, angels serve as warriors. Warrior angels do battle against God's foes, as described in Daniel and Revelation. They also protect God's people. In 2 Kings 6, we read how the prophet Elisha's servant was alarmed to discover the Syrian army had surrounded the city of Dothan and planned to capture his master. Elisha prayed for his servant's eyes to be opened. Suddenly, the servant was able to see an enormous angel army poised to protect Elisha.

Fourth, angels serve as managers. Managing angels rule the elements. They work in and through God's creation. They help maintain His order. They carry out the justice of God's court by smiting those who fail to heed the Lord's warnings and must suffer the consequences.

This vital work of angels earned them great notoriety among God's people. As the apostle Paul notes, it even led some into the "worship of angels" (Colossians 2:18). But the truth, as the author of Hebrews states, is that they are as far removed in power from the Son of God as the finite is from the infinite. Angels are emissaries from God, instruments of His grace and protection, and executors of His judgment, but they not in the same place as God or as Jesus the Son. All glory and praise for their work belong rightly to our heavenly Father.

LETTER TO THE HEBREWS

Journaling Your Response

How are you tempted to put other things above Christ when it comes to your priorities, how you spend your time, or the way you use your resources?

LESSON *two*

WHEN GOD BECAME MAN
Hebrews 2:1–18

Getting Started

It's easier to get through a difficult time if you have someone in your life who has been through something similar and overcome it. How has someone specifically helped you in this way?

Been there; done that
Support groups Al-anon

SETTING THE STAGE

Each year, as fall transitions to winter, a transformation takes place over much of the world. People begin to buy gifts for others. They decorate their houses with lights, trees, and ornaments. They make plans to gather with their family and friends. Many people go to church for the first time since Easter. Christmas touches almost everyone.

Certainly, there is an alarming amount of commercialization that goes along with the season. Yet there is also an undeniable spirit of goodwill that spreads throughout culture. On Christmas Day, the world seems to go silent for twenty-four hours, as stores close and only necessary facilities remain open. There is a global acknowledgement of something special . . . a recognition of a singular event that occurred more than 2,000 years ago.

Christians call it the Advent season—the celebration of the incarnation of Jesus Christ. *Advent* refers to the fact that Jesus came down from heaven. *Incarnation* refers to the fact that He became one of us. God's own Son took on human form. Yet the full implications of the Incarnation—*why* Jesus became a man and *what* it means for us—rarely get addressed during the Christmas season. They are far too complex to be set to music and sung as carols. Yet they are crucial to our understanding of our salvation, our purpose, and our future.

The writer of Hebrews delves into the reasons and results of the Incarnation in this next section of his letter. At first glance, his focus on Jesus' humanity seems to be a contradiction from his focus on Jesus' superiority to angels in his opening chapter. However, it quickly becomes apparent that Jesus' humanity figures prominently in His superiority to angels.

EXPLORING THE TEXT

Do Not Neglect Salvation (Hebrews 2:1–4)

> ¹ Therefore we must give the more earnest heed to the things we have heard, lest we drift away. ² For if the word spoken through

angels proved steadfast, and every transgression and disobedience received a just reward, ³ how shall we escape if we neglect so great a salvation, which at the first began to be spoken by the Lord, and was confirmed to us by those who heard Him, ⁴ God also bearing witness both with signs and wonders, with various miracles, and gifts of the Holy Spirit, according to His own will?

---

1. The Greek word translated as "drift away" literally means "to flow by," like a boat floating effortlessly away on the water. It suggests not necessarily doing something wrong but failing to take positive action. How can believers in Christ avoid this from happening (see verse 1)?

_____

_____

_____

_____

_____

_____

2. The use of the phrase "the word spoken through angels" refers to the Jewish belief that the Law had been brought to Moses by angels. The Jewish people knew from experience the importance of keeping God's original covenant. How did God emphasize the importance of the new covenant that Jesus introduced (see verses 2–4)?

_____

_____

_____

_____

_____

_____

The Son Made Lower Than Angels (Hebrews 2:5–9)

⁵ For He has not put the world to come, of which we speak, in subjection to angels. ⁶ But one testified in a certain place, saying:

> "What is man that You are mindful of him,
> Or the son of man that You take care of him?
> ⁷ You have made him a little lower than the angels;
> You have crowned him with glory and honor,
> And set him over the works of Your hands.
> ⁸ You have put all things in subjection under his feet."

For in that He put all in subjection under him, He left nothing that is not put under him. But now we do not yet see all things put under him. ⁹ But we see Jesus, who was made a little lower than the angels, for the suffering of death crowned with glory and honor, that He, by the grace of God, might taste death for everyone.

3. The writer of Hebrews continues to stress Jesus' superiority by noting that God has not put "the world to come" under the authority of angels but under the authority of Christ. How does the citation from Psalm 8:4–6 help to support this claim (see verses 6–8)?

4. The phrase "son of man" and references to Jesus being made "a little lower than the angels" emphasize Christ's humanity—that He is one of us. Why was it necessary for Jesus to be made lower than the angels for a time (see verses 8–9)? *To experience & know humanity*

Bringing Many Sons to Glory (Hebrews 2:10–13)

¹⁰ For it was fitting for Him, for whom are all things and by whom are all things, in bringing many sons to glory, to make the captain of their salvation perfect through sufferings. ¹¹ For both He who sanctifies and those who are being sanctified are all of one, for which reason He is not ashamed to call them brethren, ¹² saying:

"I will declare Your name to My brethren;
In the midst of the assembly I will sing praise to You."

¹³ And again:

"I will put My trust in Him."

And again:

"Here am I and the children whom God has given Me."

LETTER TO THE HEBREWS

5. Jesus is depicted in this passage as the "captain" of our salvation. He has not only made salvation possible but has also shown us the way to obtain it. What did this require from Christ? How does God now view us because of Jesus' sacrifice (see verses 10–11)?

One in Christ

6. The passages the writer cites in verses 12–13 are from Psalm 22:22 (which Jesus quoted from the cross) and from Isaiah 8:17–18. Jesus is saying that He calls us His brothers and sisters. What does this say about the way that God now views us?

We are His children!

A Merciful and Faithful High Priest (Hebrews 2:14–18)

¹⁴ Inasmuch then as the children have partaken of flesh and blood, He Himself likewise shared in the same, that through death He might destroy him who had the power of death, that is, the devil, ¹⁵ and

release those who through fear of death were all their lifetime subject to bondage. ¹⁶ For indeed He does not give aid to angels, but He does give aid to the seed of Abraham. ¹⁷ Therefore, in all things He had to be made like His brethren, that He might be a merciful and faithful High Priest in things pertaining to God, to make propitiation for the sins of the people. ¹⁸ For in that He Himself has suffered, being tempted, He is able to aid those who are tempted.

7. The comment that we have "partaken of flesh and blood" simply refers to our humanity—that we are composed of flesh and blood. Jesus "likewise shared" in that humanity. What did this allow Him to accomplish through His death (see verses 14–15)?

Destroy power of death

8. According to Jewish tradition, the high priest had to be chosen from among the community he served. In order for Jesus to become our high priest, He had to become one of us. Why does His incarnation make Him ideal to fill the role of high priest (see verses 17–18)?

His suffering v. 3

Reviewing the Story

The author of Hebrews reveals Jesus' superiority to angels by focusing on His humanity. God made promises to humans that were never given to angels. When sin interfered with the fulfillment of those promises, Jesus became one of us to do what we couldn't do on our own. By taking physical form, He temporarily made Himself lower than the angels, who are spiritual beings. Yet the glory and honor of His sacrifice places Him far above the angels. As a result, we have a fellow brother and high priest who can empathize with our situation.

9. Why must we never neglect the salvation that we have been given (see Hebrews 2:1–4)?

Lest we drift away

10. How did Jesus' incarnation, which temporarily made Him "a little lower than the angels," ultimately give Him power and glory far above the angels (see Hebrews 2:7–8)?

Everything was under his power

11. What did Jesus' incarnation allow Him to do on our behalf (see Hebrews 2:10–11? *brethren*

12. Why was it important for Jesus to experience suffering and temptation (see Hebrews 2:18)? *He became able to help those who suffered to were tempted.*

Applying the Message

13. How can you prevent the truth about Jesus' incarnation—and the implications of it—from "drifting away" in your own life?

14. How does it help to know that Jesus can identify with your temptations and can aid you in getting through them? How will that affect the way you pray today?

Reflecting on the Meaning

The letter of Hebrews opened with the claim that Jesus is superior to the angels. God placed Him at His right hand of the throne and gave Him authority over everything in heaven and on the earth. But Jesus also intentionally *lowered* Himself below the angels. He became a flesh-and-blood human being. In doing so, He accomplished at least four things on our behalf.

First, Jesus regained our destiny. "Jesus . . . was made a little lower than the angels . . . that He, by the grace of God, might taste death for everyone" (Hebrews 2:9). God created the first humans to live forever. He gave them honor and glory. He gave them dominion over His creation. He put them at the center of His creative work. He intended for them to rule the earth (see Genesis 1:26–28). But Adam's sinful rebellion postponed God's original intention. So God intervened on our behalf. Through the ultimate sacrifice of Christ, the Second Adam, all that was lost will be regained. We will rule and reign with Christ on this earth.

Second, Jesus recovered our unity. "It was fitting for [God] . . . in bringing many sons to glory, to make the captain of their salvation perfect through sufferings" (Hebrews 2:10). Our union with God was shattered by the sin of Adam and Eve. Jesus' death on the cross was the only thing that could restore our perfect unity with our heavenly Father. Through Jesus' sacrifice, He has made us His brothers and sisters.

Third, Jesus freed us from captivity. "Inasmuch then as the children have partaken of flesh and blood, He Himself likewise shared in the same, that through death He might destroy him who had the power of death . . . and release those who through fear of death were all their lifetime subject to bondage" (Hebrews 2:14–15). Jesus confronted Satan and robbed him of his greatest weapon. As a result, we no longer have to fear death.

Fourth, Jesus related to us in our frailty. "In all things He had to be made like His brethren, that He might be a merciful and faithful High Priest in things pertaining to God, to make propitiation for the sins of the people" (Hebrews 2:17). Jesus became a man to help us in our weakness. He is *merciful* in that He understands us and our weaknesses. He is *faithful* in that He, as God, will make His mercy available for all who request it.

We will all face trials, tribulations, and temptations. At such times, it is encouraging to know that we serve a God who has been where we are and understands what we are facing. We have this assurance because Jesus became flesh-and-blood just as we are.

Journaling Your Response

What trials, tribulations, and temptations are you facing today that you need to bring to Jesus—knowing that He will be merciful toward you and faithful to help you?

LESSON *three*

A SOFT HEART TOWARD GOD

Hebrews 3:1–19

Getting Started

What are the spiritual symptoms of a hard heart?

Setting the Stage

We live in a society that is familiar with warning signs. When you drive down the road, signs tell you to slow down, or watch out for a sharp turn that is approaching, or let you know that your lane will be ending soon and you better move over. If you've seen a commercial for pharmaceutical products, you know the warnings and legal disclaimers can take up half the running time. Warnings even appear on cups of coffee, informing us that the contents are hot.

This next section in Hebrews serves as a kind of "warning sticker." As you will recall, the original recipients of the letter were Jewish Christians who were undergoing persecution for their beliefs and were tempted to return to their former ways. They were in peril of hardening their hearts to the message of salvation and returning to life under the Old Testament law. They needed to be warned of the danger through a reminder of the consequences their Jewish ancestors suffered in the past because of this same kind of hard-heartedness.

One example of this is the story of the Israelites preparing to enter into the Promised Land. The Lord had promised to give the region of Canaan to them. However, when the people heard negative reports from ten spies who had been sent to investigate the land, their hearts faltered, and they chose not to trust in God's promises. The Israelites refused to claim what God had given to them! In doing so, they forfeited the rest that He had intended for them. Instead, they spent forty more years wandering in the wilderness (see Numbers 14).

The author of Hebrews sees this same attitude at work in the Jewish believers of his day. They are in danger of rebelling against God by refusing the salvation that Jesus Christ has freely offered to them. They are on the verge of forfeiting the rest that the Lord God intends for them to have. They are perilously close to repeating the mistakes of their Israelite ancestors from the past. These believers need to do what those ancestors did not do—soften their hearts to God and choose to trust and obey Him.

Exploring the Text

The Son Was Faithful (Hebrews 3:1–6)

¹ Therefore, holy brethren, partakers of the heavenly calling, consider the Apostle and High Priest of our confession, Christ Jesus, ² who was faithful to Him who appointed Him, as Moses also was faithful in all His house. ³ For this One has been counted worthy of more glory than Moses, inasmuch as He who built the house has more honor than the house. ⁴ For every house is built by someone, but He who built all things is God. ⁵ And Moses indeed was faithful in all His house as a servant, for a testimony of those things which would be spoken afterward, ⁶ but Christ as a Son over His own house, whose house we are if we hold fast the confidence and the rejoicing of the hope firm to the end.

---

1. Jesus is superior to heavenly angels, but He is also superior to earthly leaders—including prominent figures such as Moses and Joshua. This comparison is made by acknowledging Moses' revered status and role. How is Moses' legacy summarized (see verses 1–2)?

_____
_____
_____
_____
_____
_____
_____
_____
_____
_____
_____
_____

LETTER TO THE HEBREWS

2. The writer notes in verses 3–5 that Moses was a faithful servant *in* God's "house," which here represents the nation of Israel. But in verse 6, note that Jesus is a Son *over* His "house," which here represents the church. What point is he making about Jesus' superiority to Moses? What is necessary to be counted among Jesus' own house?

Be Faithful (Hebrews 3:7–11)

⁷ Therefore, as the Holy Spirit says:

> "Today, if you will hear His voice,
> ⁸ Do not harden your hearts as in the rebellion,
> In the day of trial in the wilderness,
> ⁹ Where your fathers tested Me, tried Me,
> And saw My works forty years.
> ¹⁰ Therefore I was angry with that generation,
> And said, 'They always go astray in their heart,
> And they have not known My ways.'
> ¹¹ So I swore in My wrath,
> 'They shall not enter My rest.'"

3. The writer's reflections on Moses lead him to reflect on the rebellion of the Israelites in the wilderness, who refused to heed God's voice and enter into the Promised Land. He sets up his exhortation by first quoting the text of Psalm 95:7–11. What does he say the Israelites did in the rebellion—in spite of what they had seen (see verses 7–9)?

4. The passage goes on to explore the results of the Israelites' rebellion. How did God react to their actions? What were the consequences for the people (see verses 9–11)?

Warning Against Disobedience (Hebrews 3:12–15)

¹² Beware, brethren, lest there be in any of you an evil heart of unbelief in departing from the living God; ¹³ but exhort one another daily, while it is called "Today," lest any of you be hardened through

the deceitfulness of sin. ¹⁴ For we have become partakers of Christ if we hold the beginning of our confidence steadfast to the end, ¹⁵ while it is said:

> "Today, if you will hear His voice,
> Do not harden your hearts as in the rebellion."

---

5. Remember the intended audience of this letter. How does the writer compare their attitude to that of the ancient Israelites (see verses 12–13)?

6. The Israelites discovered the hard way that the opportunity to obey God must be embraced "today"—for tomorrow may be too late. What are believers likewise urged to do on a daily basis in order to keep their hearts tender toward God (see verses 13–15)?

A SOFT HEART TOWARD GOD

Failure of the Wilderness Wanderers (Hebrews 3:16–19)

¹⁶ For who, having heard, rebelled? Indeed, was it not all who came out of Egypt, led by Moses? ¹⁷ Now with whom was He angry forty years? Was it not with those who sinned, whose corpses fell in the wilderness? ¹⁸ And to whom did He swear that they would not enter His rest, but to those who did not obey? ¹⁹ So we see that they could not enter in because of unbelief.

7. The warning to the readers is to not harden their hearts and rebel against God as their ancestors once did in the wilderness. The point is emphasized in this passage by asking them to consider those who chose to disobey God at Kadesh. Who is included in this group? What do you think is the application for us (see verses 16–17)?

_____
_____
_____
_____
_____
_____
_____
_____
_____
_____
_____
_____
_____

8. The verb translated as "did not obey" used at the end of verse 18 is a strong phrase that means "obstinacy." The redeemed children of Israel had committed a grave sin by refusing to respond to God's call to enter the Promised Land. What is the implied warning here to the readers of this letter (see verses 18–19)?

Reviewing the Story

The author of Hebrews reaches back into Jewish history to warn his readers about the dangers of hardening their hearts and refusing to obey God. He makes this warning by quoting from Psalm 95, written by a psalmist who also reached back into Jewish history to warn *his* readers about the dangers of repeating their ancestors' mistake at Kadesh. The key theme for each author—and for us today—is that those who harden their hearts and refuse to trust in God lose out on the "rest" that He has planned for them.

9. What trait, modeled by both Jesus and Moses, is essential to all "partakers of the heavenly calling" (see Hebrews 3:1–2)?

10. What are the God-ordained consequences for those who go "astray in their heart" (see Hebrews 3:10–11)?

11. What does it mean to be a partaker of Christ (see Hebrews 3:14)?

12. What kept the Israelites from entering into God's rest (see Hebrews 3:18–19)?

Applying the Message

13. What are some of the "warning stickers" that God has provided in your life?

14. What are some things you have learned from the example of others—both their successes and failures—that has helped you stay dedicated to God?

Reflecting on the Meaning

At the heart of this section of Hebrews is the idea of finishing strong and staying obedient to the glorious end. This is a quest that believers in Christ must pursue *together*. The encouragement and support that we receive from our community of faith can bolster our confidence and motivate us to remain obedient. By the same token, when hard-heartedness and unbelief get a toehold in a community of faith, they can spread quickly.

As a case in point, we are urged to consider the example of the Israelites. They had witnessed God perform many miracles on their behalf and provide for them in the desert. But when it came time to enter into the Promised Land, they allowed the unbelief of a few individuals to influence their trust in Him. Instead of listening to leaders like Joshua and Caleb, who said, "If the Lord delights in us, then He will lead us into this land and give it to us" (Numbers 14:8), they listened to the naysayers and allowed negativity, grumbling, and complaining to take over the entire nation. As a result, they missed out on God's blessing.

Just think of how different things might have been if the people had instead encouraged one another to trust in the Lord. They would have entered into the Promised Land immediately at Kadesh instead of being forced to wander aimlessly for forty years. They would have experienced the rest that God had promised to provide without the delay. They would have served as an example to future generations of the blessings in obeying God. But instead, when the way grew dark and the future uncertain, they decided to listen to the voice of doubt.

The author of Hebrews implores us to make a different choice. "Today, if you will hear His voice, do not harden your hearts as in the rebellion" (Hebrews 3:7–8). When our way grows dark and our future seems uncertain, we *can* choose to remain open to God, listen to His voice, and believe that He will guide us forward. We do this by staying engaged with a godly community of believers. We receive encouragement from them to persevere. And we avoid prolonged times of isolation, when the enemy can plant his lies into our minds.

Journaling Your Response

How can you encourage a fellow believer to stay strong and faithful when the going gets tough?

LESSON *four*

JESUS IS ALL YOU NEED
Hebrews 4:1–5:14

GETTING STARTED

What comes to mind when you consider the word *priest*?

Setting the Stage

No matter who we are or what we have been through in this life, there will come a time when we will feel that nobody can understand our situation. We will ache for someone to whom we can turn to address the deep needs we feel in our soul. This next section in the letter of Hebrews is all about that Someone who can identify with us and help us in our time of need.

The author of Hebrews speaks of Him as our "great High Priest" and identifies Him as "Jesus the Son of God" (4:14). The fact that Jesus "has passed through the heavens" and become one of us has two important implications for us today. The first is that He can *sympathize with us in our times of weakness* (see verse 15). The word *sympathize* is made up of two Greek words meaning "with" and "suffer." The idea is that Jesus not only sees our suffering from the outside but also *enters into our suffering* and makes it His own.

Jesus actually shares the experience of our suffering! He became a man, so He is able to understand our human limitations. He knows how it feels to be exhausted, disappointed, rejected, abandoned, and in agony. He has experienced every emotion that we feel. There is nothing we can go through in this life that He has not already encountered at a deeper level.

A second implication of Jesus-becoming-man is that He can *strengthen us in our times of temptation* (see verse 15). Some may argue that because Jesus never sinned, He never really understood temptation. But the reverse is true. We are the ones who do not understand how intense temptation can get, because we say yes to sin before Satan has thrown all his weapons of temptation at us! Jesus said no as Satan hurled every arrow in his quiver.

Jesus, the Son of God, resisted until He broke Satan's power. He did not sin, yet His temptations were all the more terrible because He endured them to the extreme. As we will see in this study, that is why He is the perfect high priest to help us when we are tempted.

Exploring the Text

The Promise of Rest (Hebrews 4:1–10)

¹ Therefore, since a promise remains of entering His rest, let us fear lest any of you seem to have come short of it. ² For indeed the gospel was preached to us as well as to them; but the word which they heard did not profit them, not being mixed with faith in those who heard it. ³ For we who have believed do enter that rest, as He has said:

> "So I swore in My wrath,
> 'They shall not enter My rest,' "

although the works were finished from the foundation of the world. ⁴ For He has spoken in a certain place of the seventh day in this way: "And God rested on the seventh day from all His works"; ⁵ and again in this place: "They shall not enter My rest."

⁶ Since therefore it remains that some must enter it, and those to whom it was first preached did not enter because of disobedience, ⁷ again He designates a certain day, saying in David, "Today," after such a long time, as it has been said:

> "Today, if you will hear His voice,
> Do not harden your hearts."

⁸ For if Joshua had given them rest, then He would not afterward have spoken of another day. ⁹ There remains therefore a rest for the people of God. ¹⁰ For he who has entered His rest has himself also ceased from his works as God did from His.

---

1. The author of Hebrews has just concluded a summary of the Israelites' failure in the wilderness and their rebellion against God.

LETTER TO THE HEBREWS

He will now apply the message to his readers, noting "the gospel" (or "good news") was preached to the Israelites, but it "did not profit them." In other words, the Israelites were given the "good news" from God—the promise of rest in Canaan—but they did not receive it. What was the reason for this (see verses 1–5)?

2. However, "a promise remains" of entering into God's rest. This promise was not fulfilled when the Israelites were able to take the land of Canaan, for under the rule of the judges they did not experience the rest they had hoped to receive. So what kind of "rest" is the author referring to here? How do believers in Christ receive it (see verses 6–10)?

The Word Discovers Our Condition (Hebrews 4:11–16)

¹¹ Let us therefore be diligent to enter that rest, lest anyone fall according to the same example of disobedience. ¹² For the word of God is living and powerful, and sharper than any two-edged sword, piercing even to the division of soul and spirit, and of joints and marrow, and is a discerner of the thoughts and intents of the heart. ¹³ And there is no creature hidden from His sight, but all things are naked and open to the eyes of Him to whom we must give account.

¹⁴ Seeing then that we have a great High Priest who has passed through the heavens, Jesus the Son of God, let us hold fast our

confession. ¹⁵ For we do not have a High Priest who cannot sympathize with our weaknesses, but was in all points tempted as we are, yet without sin. ¹⁶ Let us therefore come boldly to the throne of grace, that we may obtain mercy and find grace to help in time of need.

---

3. The writer of Hebrews has quoted several times from passages in the Old Testament to make his arguments and defend his points. He now turns to reflect on the power of that very Scripture. How does he describe the Word of God? What dynamic impact does it have on those who choose to be exposed to it (see verses 11–13)?

_____
_____
_____
_____

4. The point has been made that Jesus is greater than Old Testament prophets, greater than leaders like Moses and Joshua, and greater than angels. Now the discussion turns to how Jesus, and the new covenant He instituted, is greater than the old priestly system under the old covenant. What is Jesus, as our high priest, able to do for us? What can we now do, when it comes to meeting God, that even most of the Old Testament priests could not (see verses 14–16)?

_____
_____
_____
_____

A Priest Forever (Hebrews 5:1–8)

¹ For every high priest taken from among men is appointed for men in things pertaining to God, that he may offer both gifts and sacrifices

for sins. ² He can have compassion on those who are ignorant and going astray, since he himself is also subject to weakness. ³ Because of this he is required as for the people, so also for himself, to offer sacrifices for sins. ⁴ And no man takes this honor to himself, but he who is called by God, just as Aaron was.

⁵ So also Christ did not glorify Himself to become High Priest, but it was He who said to Him:

"You are My Son,
Today I have begotten You."

⁶ As He also says in another place:

"You are a priest forever
According to the order of Melchizedek";

⁷ who, in the days of His flesh, when He had offered up prayers and supplications, with vehement cries and tears to Him who was able to save Him from death, and was heard because of His godly fear, ⁸ though He was a Son, yet He learned obedience by the things which He suffered.

---

5. The author of Hebrews, having introduced the theme that Jesus is our "greater" and "better" high priest, now constructs his argument as to why this is true and how Christ fits that role. How did Jesus meet the requirements to be a high priest (see verses 1–6)?

6. The writer returns to the first qualification of Jesus' priesthood—His ability to represent God's people—by stating that Jesus' earthly prayers provides evidence of His humanity. What kinds of prayers did Jesus pray? How do these prayers reveal that Jesus was a human being just like the rest of us (see verses 7–8)?

_____

_____

_____

_____

_____

_____

_____

_____

Spiritual Immaturity (Hebrews 5:9–14)

⁹ And having been perfected, He became the author of eternal salvation to all who obey Him, ¹⁰ called by God as High Priest "according to the order of Melchizedek," ¹¹ of whom we have much to say, and hard to explain, since you have become dull of hearing.

¹² For though by this time you ought to be teachers, you need someone to teach you again the first principles of the oracles of God; and you have come to need milk and not solid food. ¹³ For everyone who partakes only of milk is unskilled in the word of righteousness, for he is a babe. ¹⁴ But solid food belongs to those who are of full age, that is, those who by reason of use have their senses exercised to discern both good and evil.

7. The phrase "having been perfected" does not refer to moral perfection but to Jesus' ability to perfectly fulfill His earthly mission.

How is that mission summarized in verses 9–10? Why were the readers having a hard time grasping this truth (see verse 11)?

8. The contention is that the recipients should have already grasped these fundamental truths about the Christian faith. How is the spiritual condition of these believers described? What does "solid food" represent in this sense (see verses 12–14)?

Reviewing the Story

The author of Hebrews continues his plea for his Jewish-Christian audience to not forsake their faith by reminding them of God's promise of rest to the Israelites. This is a rest that was not fulfilled during the time of their ancestors but is available "today" to those who choose to follow Christ. He then points out that Jesus is uniquely qualified to be our high priest because he can identify with us (He was human) and received a direct commission from God. The author challenges his readers to put more effort into understanding these truths about Jesus' priesthood. He wants them to experience the full blessings of it and teach others about it.

9. What is the difference in the response between those who embrace the promise of God's rest and those who forfeit it (see Hebrews 4:1–3)?

10. What should be our reaction to having a high priest who has passed through the heavens, can sympathize with our weaknesses, and was tempted as we are (see Hebrews 4:16)?

11. What did the Old Testament priests have to do that Jesus did not (see Hebrews 5:3)?

12. What is the difference between "milk" and "solid food" Christians (see Hebrews 5:12–14)?

Applying the Message

13. The Word of God is living, powerful, and sharper than any two-edged sword. How has this been true in your life? What recent truths have you discovered in the Bible?

14. Jesus understands everything that you have gone through or will go through in this life. What needs do you boldly need to bring to Him at the throne of grace?

Reflecting on the Meaning

The privilege of having Jesus as our high priest comes with tremendous responsibility. In addition to making appeals for us before the throne of God, Jesus stands ready to guide, nourish, strengthen, advise, and encourage us. Our job is to take advantage of that opportunity and continue to grow and mature, from our first step with Him to our very last.

The author of Hebrews identifies the way we do this: "Let us hold fast our confession" (Hebrews 4:14). For his Jewish readers, holding fast to their confession meant making their break from Judaism known publicly. This kind of confession was not done lightly. There were risks and repercussions. It meant they would be subjected to taunts, blacklisting, and threats.

Modern readers of Hebrews are called to do no less. Our profession of faith goes far beyond verbally affirming the gospel message—it must impact the way we live. When we hold fast to our confession, we advertise our faith to the world. We allow it to define who we are and what we do. Beyond that, when we hold fast to our confession, we reconcile ourselves to the consequences of identifying with Christ, come what may.

As we have seen, the majority of the Israelites rebelled against God at Kadesh and did not enter into the Promised Land. But there were two men who held fast to their profession of faith in God: Joshua and Caleb. These two men didn't downplay the obstacles that lay ahead when they returned from their spying mission in the Promised Land. But they were eager to tackle those challenges because they trusted in God and wanted to experience His rest.

Joshua eventually led the children of the faithless generation of the Israelites into Canaan. Caleb entered the Promised Land as well. Even though he is mentioned in less than thirty verses in the entire Bible, in five of those verses we're given all we need to know about him: "He wholly followed the LORD" (Numbers 32:12; Deuteronomy 1:36; Joshua 14:8, 9, 14).

This is how we likewise hold fast to our confession. We *wholly* follow our great high priest. We go where He leads—and we let the world know that we belong to Him.

LETTER TO THE HEBREWS

Journaling Your Response

What does holding fast to your confession look like in your life?

LESSON *five*
THE ANCHOR OF HOPE
Hebrews 6:1–20

Getting Started

What are some things that cause you to have hope in your life?

God moments
God stories

Setting the Stage

There are some historians and social scientists today who believe that our modern culture has fewer spiritual resources to draw from than at any other time in our Western cultural history. Many attribute this to our culture forsaking its spiritual roots, preferring instead a secular society that rarely gives a nod to spiritual values. As a result, many feel that our culture has failed to provide answers to questions of purpose, meaning, and destiny.

In other words, our culture has failed to provide us with *some reason for hope*. In this next section of Hebrews, we find this is the same situation in which many of the early Jewish Christians found themselves. They were under intense pressure from the society and culture around them to revert to their former ways in Judaism. Many were losing hope and giving up their faith in Christ. The writer of Hebrews, in no uncertain terms, tells them that this is a bad idea—that there is danger in not progressing in their walk with Jesus.

Yet he does not want to just leave them with a warning. So instead, he reminds them that they *do* have hope. They have "an anchor of the soul, both sure and steadfast" (Hebrews 6:19), and this anchor is none other than Jesus. They had received a wonderful grace of God that had fallen upon them like rain from the heavens. But if they chose not to *receive* that grace, they would just end up missing out on God's best for their lives.

Like these Jewish Christians, we need to receive that grace. We need to hold fast to Jesus as our anchor. We need to completely trust in Him and put our faith wholly in Him—not in the things of this world. For we all desperately need the hope that only He can provide.

Exploring the Text

The Peril of Not Progressing (Hebrews 6:1–6)

> ¹ Therefore, leaving the discussion of the elementary principles of Christ, let us go on to perfection, not laying again the foundation

of repentance from dead works and of faith toward God, ² of the doctrine of baptisms, of laying on of hands, of resurrection of the dead, and of eternal judgment. ³ And this we will do if God permits.

⁴ For it is impossible for those who were once enlightened, and have tasted the heavenly gift, and have become partakers of the Holy Spirit, ⁵ and have tasted the good word of God and the powers of the age to come, ⁶ if they fall away, to renew them again to repentance, since they crucify again for themselves the Son of God, and put Him to an open shame.

---

1. The author of Hebrews has just implored his readers to move on from the spiritual "milk" they received as babes in Christ and take up more solid spiritual "food." The word he uses for *leaving* in the opening of this passage conveys the same idea—it might be better translated as "moving on." What are these elementary principles about Christ from which we should "move on" after we have laid the foundation of our faith (see verses 1–3)?

2. The statement "those who were once enlightened" likely refers back to the discussion on the rebellious generation of the Israelites who refused to enter into the Promised Land (see Hebrews 4:1–10). The Israelites had received the light of God, tasted His gifts and partaken with Him, yet they could not ultimately receive God's rest due to their falling away. How does this same reality apply to believers (see Hebrews 6:4–6)?

A Better Estimate (Hebrews 6:7–12)

> ⁷ For the earth which drinks in the rain that often comes upon it, and bears herbs useful for those by whom it is cultivated, receives blessing from God; ⁸ but if it bears thorns and briers, it is rejected and near to being cursed, whose end is to be burned.
>
> ⁹ But, beloved, we are confident of better things concerning you, yes, things that accompany salvation, though we speak in this manner. ¹⁰ For God is not unjust to forget your work and labor of love which you have shown toward His name, in that you have ministered

to the saints, and do minister. ¹¹ And we desire that each one of you show the same diligence to the full assurance of hope until the end, ¹² that you do not become sluggish, but imitate those who through faith and patience inherit the promises.

---

3. The agricultural analogy used in this passage brings to mind Jesus' parable of the sower (see Matthew 13:1–9, 18–23) and parable of the weeds (see Matthew 13:24–30). In this letter, however, bearing useful herbs signifies spiritual growth. What two outcomes does the author envision, based on whether spiritual growth occurs (see verses 7–8)?

4. The writer of Hebrews has spoken in detail about missing out on God's promises and His rest, but this is not to imply that his readers have lost their salvation. Rather, he is providing a stern warning for them to not rest on their spiritual laurels. What strategies does he suggest in this regard for maintaining diligence and hope (see verses 9–12)?

God's Infallible Purpose in Christ (Hebrews 6:13–16)

> [13] For when God made a promise to Abraham, because He could swear by no one greater, He swore by Himself, [14] saying, "Surely blessing I will bless you, and multiplying I will multiply you." [15] And so, after he had patiently endured, he obtained the promise. [16] For men indeed swear by the greater, and an oath for confirmation is for them an end of all dispute.

5. The use of the word *for* links this passage back to the people just discussed—those who inherit God's promises through faith and perseverance. The readers are assured, through the retelling of the story of Abraham, that these promises from God will come to pass. What promise did God make to Abraham? How did He secure this promise (see verses 13–14)?

6. In a courtroom, witnesses take an oath to "tell the truth, the whole truth, and nothing but the truth, so help me God." The oath involves the witnesses swearing to a greater power than themselves (God), with the understanding that breaking such an oath will incur a sanction (the federal crime of perjury.) In this section of Hebrews, we read that God made an oath to Abraham regarding His promise. What did He "swear by" (see verses 13–16)?

_____

_____

_____

_____

_____

The Anchor of the Soul (Hebrews 6:17–20)

> [17] Thus God, determining to show more abundantly to the heirs of promise the immutability of His counsel, confirmed it by an oath, [18] that by two immutable things, in which it is impossible for God to lie, we might have strong consolation, who have fled for refuge to lay hold of the hope set before us.
>
> [19] This hope we have as an anchor of the soul, both sure and steadfast, and which enters the Presence behind the veil, [20] where the forerunner has entered for us, even Jesus, having become High Priest forever according to the order of Melchizedek.

7. We now arrive at the apex of the argument: God does not lie, so if He has declared something on oath, we can be assured that it will come to pass. How does this knowledge lead to us having "hope"—the assurance of eternal life (see verses 17–18)?

_____

_____

_____

_____

_____

8. This section closes with a reflection on the role of Jesus as our high priest. How does our faith in Christ serve as an "anchor" for our soul? What can we be assured that Jesus, as our high priest, is doing on our behalf (see verses 19–20)?

Reviewing the Story

The author of Hebrews builds on his theme of spiritual maturity that he introduced in chapter 5. He makes an important connection between our growth as believers and the hope we experience. When our growth stagnates, so does our hope. The writer then assures his readers that God remembers the work done in His name. He urges us to continue that work until the end of our lives. The hope that results from continued faithfulness is rooted in God's oath to us. The fact that God swore that oath to Himself means that our hope is secure forever!

9. What are some dangers of not growing in our Christian faith (see Hebrews 6:1–6)?

10. What is a good strategy for avoiding sluggishness in our spiritual life (see Hebrews 6:12)?

11. What did Abraham have to do before he obtained God's promise (see Hebrews 6:15)?

12. How can we know that God will fulfill His promises to us (see Hebrews 6:18)?

Applying the Message

13. What is the biggest challenge you face when it comes to growing in your faith?

14. How does it impact you to know that God has—and always will—keep His promises?

Reflecting on the Meaning

At the end of this section of Hebrews, the author provides a picture to help his readers grasp God's faithfulness. God's faithfulness to keep His promise gives us hope, and this hope is "an anchor of the soul"

(Hebrews 6:19). Now, the way that we use the word *hope* today is entirely different from how the biblical writers used the word. For instance, we may say, "I hope it doesn't rain tomorrow." Such a hope for clear weather is baseless, except for a weatherman's prediction. The weather can change; it is ultimately unpredictable.

But hope in the Bible is a certainty and something on which we can build our lives. Indeed, hope in the Bible is as solid as an *anchor*—something people in the biblical world knew a lot about. The image is of a ship being tossed in a storm, with only a heavy anchor and a strong rope keeping the craft from being dashed on the rocks. In the Christian's life, that anchor is Jesus Himself. He keeps us steady, safe, and secure in the roughest storms.

Even more, this anchor is not fixed on the bottom of the ocean, but is in the presence of God "behind the veil" (verse 19), which refers to the heavenly and holy throne of God. Jesus has gone ahead of us as "the forerunner" (verse 20) to anchor us to God forever. He has "become High Priest forever" (verse 20)—the only one who could enter the presence of God on our behalf. He is our anchor, our promise, and our faithful high priest in the presence of God.

The term *forerunner* refers to a kind of craft used in ancient times. Sandbars would often prevent ships entering a harbor at low tide, so a lighter boat, called a forerunner, would be used to row out to the ship. The forerunner would pick up the ship's anchor and then carry it back across the sandbar where it could be dropped inside the harbor. At high tide, the larger ship could then sail into the safety of the harbor, where its anchor was holding it fast.

In that sense, Jesus is our "forerunner" into the presence of God, where He holds fast our connection until we arrive there. So, when life gets turbulent and we are buffeted by winds and waves of circumstance, we must remember that we are connected to this anchor of our soul. He has removed the barrier that once separated us from God's presence (see Matthew 27:51). Access to God is now available for all through Jesus—who has gone before us.

Journaling Your Response

In what area of your life do you most need hope right now?

LESSON *six*

KING AND HIGH PRIEST
Hebrews 7:1–28

Getting Started

Jesus is both a king and high priest in the sense that He is the sovereign authority in your life but also intercedes before God on your behalf. How do you see these two roles in your life?

Setting the Stage

He has been alluded to several times now in Hebrews. He is one of the most mysterious figures in the Bible. In the Old Testament, his name appears only twice: once in Genesis 14:18–20, and again in Psalm 110:4. In both instances, he is described as a priest. In the Genesis account, he is also described as a king. His name? Melchizedek . . . the priest-king.

The shadowy figure must have fascinated the writer of Hebrews. In this next section of his letter, he draws on the scant information provided about this man to make a compelling case that Melchizedek is a picture of Jesus Christ and His priestly ministry. He begins by noting the name Melchizedek means "king of righteousness." Melchizedek was the king of Salem (Jerusalem), which means he was the *king of peace.* The fact he held the double role of king and priest was unique in Jewish history. As king, he had power with men. As priest, he had power with God. He brought together righteousness and peace, just as Christ did centuries later.

Abraham encountered Melchizedek after defeating a coalition of kings (see Genesis 14:1–17). The patriarch was carrying home the spoils of war. While the Bible offers few details of their encounter, we do know that Abraham recognized in Melchizedek a power far greater than his own. He paid tribute to the priest-king by offering him a tithe (see verses 18–20).

The greatness of Abraham underscores the greatness of Melchizedek. Abraham was perhaps the greatest man on earth at the time, yet still he paid tithes to Melchizedek. Melchizedek's greatness can be seen in the fact that he expected Abraham to give him tithes and then accepted them when they were offered. He also blessed Abraham. As the text of Hebrews points out, the lesser is always blessed by the greater.

By linking Jesus to Melchizedek, the writer dramatically expands the scope of what a high priest can be—and what he can do in our own lives.

Exploring the Text

The King of Righteousness (Hebrews 7:1–7)

¹ For this Melchizedek, king of Salem, priest of the Most High God, who met Abraham returning from the slaughter of the kings and blessed him, ² to whom also Abraham gave a tenth part of all, first

KING AND HIGH PRIEST

being translated "king of righteousness," and then also king of Salem, meaning "king of peace," ³ without father, without mother, without genealogy, having neither beginning of days nor end of life, but made like the Son of God, remains a priest continually.

⁴ Now consider how great this man was, to whom even the patriarch Abraham gave a tenth of the spoils. ⁵ And indeed those who are of the sons of Levi, who receive the priesthood, have a commandment to receive tithes from the people according to the law, that is, from their brethren, though they have come from the loins of Abraham; ⁶ but he whose genealogy is not derived from them received tithes from Abraham and blessed him who had the promises. ⁷ Now beyond all contradiction the lesser is blessed by the better.

---

1. The author of Hebrews begins by making some interesting conclusions about Melchizedek based on the scant information provided in the Old Testament. In the Genesis account, Melchizedek appears on the scene quickly and disappears just as abruptly. We are given his name and office, but no additional details about his family or background. In literary terms, he is thus "without father, without mother, without genealogy." How does the author use these conclusions about Melchizedek to portray him as a model of Christ (see verses 1–3)?

_____
_____
_____
_____
_____
_____

2. Abraham was considered one of the greatest heroes of the Jewish faith. He was the founding father of the Jewish people and held in high esteem for his absolute faith in God. Only Moses and David were placed on equal ground among the Jewish people. But the argument being made here is that Melchizedek was *greater* than Abraham. What evidence is provided in the passage to support this claim (see verses 4–7)?

_____

_____

_____

_____

_____

_____

_____

Need for a New Priesthood (Hebrews 7:8–13)

> ⁸ Here mortal men receive tithes, but there he receives them, of whom it is witnessed that he lives. ⁹ Even Levi, who receives tithes, paid tithes through Abraham, so to speak, ¹⁰ for he was still in the loins of his father when Melchizedek met him.
>
> ¹¹ Therefore, if perfection were through the Levitical priesthood (for under it the people received the law), what further need was there that another priest should rise according to the order of Melchizedek, and not be called according to the order of Aaron? ¹² For the priesthood being changed, of necessity there is also a change of the law. ¹³ For He of whom these things are spoken belongs to another tribe, from which no man has officiated at the altar.

3. Melchizedek was thus superior to Abraham. In this passage, we also see that Melchizedek's priesthood was superior to the Levitical priesthood. Melchizedek was a "priest forever" (see Psalm 110:4) and received tithes from Abraham, even though this practice would not be instituted until the time of Levi, a descendant of Abraham. How does this make the order of Melchizedek's priesthood superior to the Levitical priesthood (see verses 8–10)?

4. The key argument in this passage is that a person only replaces something if it is found to be *faulty*. How did that apply to the Levitical priesthood and the Old Testament law from which it came (see verses 11–13)?

Greatness of the New Priest (Hebrews 7:14–22)

¹⁴ For it is evident that our Lord arose from Judah, of which tribe Moses spoke nothing concerning priesthood. ¹⁵ And it is yet far more evident if, in the likeness of Melchizedek, there arises another priest ¹⁶ who has come, not according to the law of a fleshly commandment, but according to the power of an endless life. ¹⁷ For He testifies:

> "You are a priest forever
> According to the order of Melchizedek."

¹⁸ For on the one hand there is an annulling of the former commandment because of its weakness and unprofitableness, ¹⁹ for the law made nothing perfect; on the other hand, there is the bringing in of a better hope, through which we draw near to God.

²⁰ And inasmuch as He was not made priest without an oath ²¹ (for they have become priests without an oath, but He with an oath by Him who said to Him:

"The LORD has sworn
And will not relent,
'You are a priest forever
According to the order of Melchizedek' "),

²² by so much more Jesus has become a surety of a better covenant.

---

5. The conclusion of the argument is that the old order of the priesthood under Aaron was imperfect and thus had to be replaced by a new order of priesthood in the likeness of Melchizedek. This new order has now appeared, with Jesus as its high priest. What are some of the reasons given as to why this order under Christ is different (see verses 14–17)?

_____
_____
_____
_____
_____
_____
_____

6. The apostle Paul wrote that "what the law could not do . . . God did by sending His own Son" (Romans 8:3). The writer of Hebrews supports this claim. Why was the former law annulled? What has Jesus' death made possible for us (see verses 18–19)?

An Unchangeable Priesthood (Hebrews 7:23–28)

²³ Also there were many priests, because they were prevented by death from continuing. ²⁴ But He, because He continues forever, has an unchangeable priesthood. ²⁵ Therefore He is also able to save to the uttermost those who come to God through Him, since He always lives to make intercession for them.

²⁶ For such a High Priest was fitting for us, who is holy, harmless, undefiled, separate from sinners, and has become higher than the heavens; ²⁷ who does not need daily, as those high priests, to offer up sacrifices, first for His own sins and then for the people's, for this He did once for all when He offered up Himself. ²⁸ For the law appoints as high priests men who have weakness, but the word of the oath, which came after the law, appoints the Son who has been perfected forever.

7. The mortality of priests under the Levitical system caused frequent turnover and change in the Levitical system. However, the eternal priesthood of Jesus is permanent and forever. What is Jesus therefore able to do for us before God (see verses 23–25)?

8. The terms "holy," "undefiled," and "separate from sinners" used in this passage emphasize Jesus' purity and sinlessness. The same was not true of the Levitical priests, who had to offer up daily sacrifices for their own sins and then for the people's sins. How does Jesus' sinlessness make Him a much more effective priest (see verses 26–28)?

Reviewing the Story

The author of Hebrews relates in this chapter how Jesus was able to replace the old and imperfect priesthood of Israel. First, Jesus came from the order of Melchizedek (which predated the Levitical priesthood) and is eternal. Second, unlike the Levitical priests, He was without sin and thus was able to fully intercede for people's sins. Third, He occupies an exalted position at the right hand of God. Jesus is the perfect intermediary between us and our heavenly Father.

KING AND HIGH PRIEST

9. What connections does the author of Hebrews draw between Melchizedek and Jesus (see Hebrews 7:1–3)?

10. What set Jesus apart from other priests (see Hebrews 7:13–14)?

11. What does Jesus, our better hope, allow us to do (see Hebrews 7:19)?

12. Why did the Old Testament law need to be changed (see Hebrews 7:28)?

Applying the Message

13. What does it mean to you that Jesus constantly intercedes on your behalf before God?

14. What is the best way to respond to Jesus' sacrifice and His intercession for you?

Reflecting on the Meaning

The author's primary point in this chapter of Hebrews is that Jesus, as our high priest, was able to do for us what the Old Testament priests could not do—and what we could not do for ourselves. But in order to fully appreciate what Jesus is able to do, we must understand what the Levitical priesthood was *not* able to do. After all, if the Levitical priesthood had been perfect, another priest would not have been needed. But God's goal of establishing an eternal relationship between Himself and us could not be accomplished through that system.

First, the Levitical priesthood could not save a person from sin. "For on the one hand there is an annulling of the former commandment because of its weakness and unprofitableness, for the law made nothing perfect" (Hebrews 7:18–19). The law had the power to reveal a person's sin, but it had no power to release a person from that sin. For this reason, the priests had to offer an endless series of sacrifices to atone for the people's sin. But when God sent Jesus into the world, he instituted not just a change in priesthood but also a change in the law. With Christ as our high priest, we are no longer under the Mosaic law.

Second, the Levitical priesthood could not bring a person into God's presence. "On the other hand, there is the bringing in of a better hope, through which we draw near to God" (verse 19). Under the old covenant, the high priest could only enter the Holy of Holies once each year on the Day of Atonement. There, the high priest engaged in a number of rituals to atone for the people's sins (see Leviticus 16). But when God instituted Jesus as our high priest, he removed the veil of separation between us. Now, with Jesus as our high priest, we can enter into God's presence and approach the very throne of grace with boldness.

Third, the Levitical priesthood could not provide a perfect sacrifice for sin. "For such a High Priest was fitting for us . . . who does not need daily, as those high priests, to offer up sacrifices, first for His own sins and then for the people's, for this He did once for all when He offered up Himself" (Hebrews 7:26–27). The Old Testament priests—even the most righteous among them—were still human and thus susceptible to sin. But when God sent Jesus as our high priest, He also provided a perfect and sinless sacrifice to forever atone for our sins.

Only Jesus Christ can save us completely. No other priest will ever be necessary. Our greater high priest is able to shepherd us all the way to glory. He is able to intercede for us at the right hand of God. He is able to come alongside us whenever we are tempted. He can sympathize with us in our weaknesses. He gives mercy and grace to help us in times of need. He will see us through every trial and difficulty. We must only remain faithful to Him.

Journaling Your Response

What is your prayer today to Jesus, your perfect, eternal, and gracious high priest?

LESSON *seven*

A NEW COVENANT
Hebrews 8:1–9:10

Getting Started

An examination of what *does not* work in life can often lead to an understanding of what *will* work in life. How have you found this to be true in your experience?

Setting the Stage

Imagine that for years you travelled to work following the same old route. The road was filled with traffic lights, often became bottlenecked, and could be hazardous because of all the potholes. But then one day, you learned that a new interstate had just been opened. Now you could zip to work in a fraction of the time it took you before.

If you had that option available, you would take it and never drive the old way again. You would rejoice in the fact that you no longer had to punish yourself with the extended driving time and tension the old route produced. Sure, you would acknowledge the old road served you well. But now that the new highway has been completed, the old one is obsolete.

So far in the book of Hebrews, the writer has made many comparisons between the "old" and the "new." He has compared the old system under the law—with its prophets, priesthood, and leaders like Moses and Joshua—to the new system under Christ. He has pointed out how the road with Jesus is superior to everything the old way had to offer. Sure, that old system had value in its time. But now it is obsolete.

In this next chapter in Hebrews, the author will now compare the old earthly tabernacle given to the Hebrew people with the new eternal tabernacle given to the followers of Christ. He will show that the first tabernacle was ordained by God, but it was limited in function in that it was an *earthly* sanctuary serviced by an *earthly* priesthood. However, the new tabernacle is unlimited in that it is a *heavenly* sanctuary under our great *eternal* High Priest.

The tabernacle was God's provision for His people on their journey from Egypt to the Promised Land. But now it is obsolete. So why would anyone want to travel that way again?

Exploring the Text

The New Priestly Service (Hebrews 8:1–6)

¹ Now this is the main point of the things we are saying: We have such a High Priest, who is seated at the right hand of the throne of the Majesty in the heavens, ² a Minister of the sanctuary and of the true tabernacle which the Lord erected, and not man.

A NEW COVENANT

³ For every high priest is appointed to offer both gifts and sacrifices. Therefore it is necessary that this One also have something to offer. ⁴ For if He were on earth, He would not be a priest, since there are priests who offer the gifts according to the law; ⁵ who serve the copy and shadow of the heavenly things, as Moses was divinely instructed when he was about to make the tabernacle. For He said, "See that you make all things according to the pattern shown you on the mountain." ⁶ But now He has obtained a more excellent ministry, inasmuch as He is also Mediator of a better covenant, which was established on better promises.

---

1. The author of Hebrews begins this chapter with a summary of what he has just discussed: we have a new High Priest who functions under a new covenant in a new tabernacle established by God. What does he say earthly high priests were appointed to do? What is thus required of our heavenly High Priest (see verses 1–3)?

2. The next point made is that Jesus was from the tribe of Judah—not Levi—and thus not eligible to serve as a priest under the earthly system. Jesus is thus a high priest under a new order. What are the traits of this new priestly ministry (see verses 4–6)?

_____

_____

_____

_____

_____

A New Covenant (Hebrews 8:7–13)

⁷ For if that first covenant had been faultless, then no place would have been sought for a second. ⁸ Because finding fault with them, He says: "Behold, the days are coming, says the Lord, when I will make a new covenant with the house of Israel and with the house of Judah—⁹ not according to the covenant that I made with their fathers in the day when I took them by the hand to lead them out of the land of Egypt; because they did not continue in My covenant, and I disregarded them, says the Lord. ¹⁰ For this is the covenant that I will make with the house of Israel after those days, says the Lord: I will put My laws in their mind and write them on their hearts; and I will be their God, and they shall be My people. ¹¹ None of them shall teach his neighbor, and none his brother, saying, 'Know the Lord,' for all shall know Me, from the least of them to the greatest of them. ¹² For I will be merciful to their unrighteousness, and their sins and their lawless deeds I will remember no more."

¹³ In that He says, "A new covenant," He has made the first obsolete. Now what is becoming obsolete and growing old is ready to vanish away.

3. The writer reiterates a point he made previously that if the old covenant (the law) had been faultless, there would be no need to replace it. However, as the prophecy he cites from Jeremiah 31:31–34 reveals, the Lord had stated that He *would* make a new covenant with His people. This covenant would be better than the one He had made with their ancestors. What was the weakness of that old covenant (see verses 7–12)?

4. The citation from Jeremiah is the longest Old Testament text found in the New Testament. Yet only *three words* are singled for further explanation: "a new covenant." What does this explanation tell us about God's attitude toward the old covenant (see verse 13)?

The Earthly Sanctuary (Hebrews 9:1–5)

¹ Then indeed, even the first covenant had ordinances of divine service and the earthly sanctuary. ² For a tabernacle was prepared: the first part, in which was the lampstand, the table, and the showbread,

which is called the sanctuary; ³ and behind the second veil, the part of the tabernacle which is called the Holiest of All, ⁴ which had the golden censer and the ark of the covenant overlaid on all sides with gold, in which were the golden pot that had the manna, Aaron's rod that budded, and the tablets of the covenant; ⁵ and above it were the cherubim of glory overshadowing the mercy seat. Of these things we cannot now speak in detail.

---

5. As previously noted, the earthly tabernacle was only a copy and shadow of the heavenly one to come. However, understanding how that earthly system operated can yield understanding about the heavenly tabernacle and our great High Priest. How did the builders and finishers of the earthly tabernacle attempt to represent the glory of the heavenly tabernacle (see verses 1–3)?

6. The innermost part of the tabernacle was called the "Holiest of All," as this was the place where the presence of God resided. In that room was the Ark of the Covenant. How is the Ark described in this passage (see verses 4–5)?

A NEW COVENANT

Limitations of the Earthly Service (Hebrews 9:6–10)

⁶ Now when these things had been thus prepared, the priests always went into the first part of the tabernacle, performing the services. ⁷ But into the second part the high priest went alone once a year, not without blood, which he offered for himself and for the people's sins committed in ignorance; ⁸ the Holy Spirit indicating this, that the way into the Holiest of All was not yet made manifest while the first tabernacle was still standing. ⁹ It was symbolic for the present time in which both gifts and sacrifices are offered which cannot make him who performed the service perfect in regard to the conscience— ¹⁰ concerned only with foods and drinks, various washings, and fleshly ordinances imposed until the time of reformation.

---

7. The discussion now moves to the earthly regulations for worship in the tabernacle. The entrance to the Holiest of All—where the presence of God resided—was restricted to one person (the high priest) once each year on the Day of Atonement. What needed to happen before that system could change (see verses 6–8)?

LETTER TO THE HEBREWS

8. The writer is careful not to suggest that the earthly rituals of the old covenant were worthless. What purpose did they serve (see verses 9–10)?

Reviewing the Story

The author of Hebrews discusses the earthly tabernacle and priestly system instituted by Moses to show what they reveal about the heavenly tabernacle and priestly system instituted by Christ. The old tabernacle was a product of the old covenant, which the Israelites made obsolete with their disobedience. The new covenant that Christ ushered in made the old tabernacle system obsolete. The barrier between God and man, as represented by the veil, was torn asunder. As a result, we have constant and immediate access to God's presence.

9. Why is Jesus' ministry more excellent than the earthly ministry of priests (see Hebrews 8:6)?

A NEW COVENANT

10. Why did Jesus have to usher in a new covenant (see Hebrews 8:7–9)?

11. What emblems were used in the old tabernacle system (see Hebrews 9:2–5)?

12. With what were the old covenant rituals primarily concerned (see Hebrews 9:9–10)?

Applying the Message

13. What might your life be like if you were still living under the old covenant?

14. How would you explain to an unbelieving friend what Jesus has done—and what He is doing right now—for those who believe in Him?

Reflecting on the Meaning

The author of Hebrews walks a fine line in chapters 8 and 9. He celebrates the glory of the earthly tabernacle while at the same time identifying its limitations. As glorious as the tabernacle was as the focus of worship for the Israelites, the entire structure suggested restriction, imperfection, limitation, and exclusion.

Average Israelites could enter the outer court of the tabernacle once a week to make a sacrifice at the altar of burnt offerings, but they could not go beyond that point. They had no access to God. Priests were chosen by lot once a week to serve in the first room of the tabernacle. They kept the seven lamps burning, stoked the coals on the altar, dropped handfuls of incense on the altar, and exchanged the bread. Yet they could not even glance into the second room, the Holiest of All, upon penalty of death. They had no access to God.

The high priest could go beyond the veil into the Holiest of All only once a year, on the Day of Atonement. His ministry beyond the veil was brief and prescribed. As soon as it was accomplished, he had to leave God's presence and face the barrier of the veil for another year.

The tabernacle was created to point toward the future. It taught that the way into God's immediate presence was not yet open. The tabernacle's physical structure, with its compartments and its veil, proclaimed this reality. The sacrifices also proclaimed it. They were imperfect and could never make a conscience clean.

However, what we must recognize, is that those limitations were not *flaws* in the plan but were the *essence* of the plan. The limitations of the old help us appreciate the wondrous glory of the new. Jesus' perfect sacrifice ended the need for any more sacrifices. It accomplished what countless animal sacrifices could not: complete atonement for our sins.

Jesus' death and resurrection ripped the veil between us and God. As long as Jesus is our high priest, we have access to God's presence any time we want it. This is especially good news for us, because Jesus is our high priest forever.

Journaling Your Response

How can you take full advantage of your access to God?

LESSON *eight*

THE GREAT MEDIATOR
Hebrews 9:11–28

Getting Started

What do you find is the best strategy for mediating a conflict between two people?

Setting the Stage

Mediators are worth their weight in gold. When conflict arises—whether political, social, or personal—mediators keep it from spiraling out of control. They urge the parties to rise above the rhetoric. They act as go-betweens for opponents who want nothing to do with each other. They bring two sides together who otherwise would walk away as combatants. Without mediators, the world would be a much more hostile place.

When the conflict is spiritual, the need for a mediator is even more important. Just consider the case that the Bible lays out against us. The apostle Paul states that our sin has made us "enemies" of God (Romans 5:10). James writes that those who have "friendship with the world" have "enmity with God" (James 4:4). We may find this difficult to believe. But if we deny the reality of our sin and its effects, we also bypass the work of Jesus.

In this chapter of Hebrews, the author—in his comprehensive way—examines the role that Jesus plays in reuniting us with God. He helps us understand that in Christ we have a perfect and true Mediator, for He possesses the nature and attributes of God and the nature and attributes of man. He is the God-man and, therefore, the only One who can righteously and perfectly bring peace to the two parties.

But Jesus goes beyond even this for us. He is not only our High Priest and Mediator but also the perfect sacrifice for our sins. Jesus' sinless state as a human enabled Him to offer Himself as a blood sacrifice before God for our sins once and for all. "But now, once at the end of the ages, He has appeared to put away sin by the sacrifice of Himself" (Hebrews 9:26).

Exploring the Text

The Heavenly Sanctuary (Hebrews 9:11–14)

> ¹¹ But Christ came as High Priest of the good things to come, with the greater and more perfect tabernacle not made with hands, that

is, not of this creation. ¹² Not with the blood of goats and calves, but with His own blood He entered the Most Holy Place once for all, having obtained eternal redemption. ¹³ For if the blood of bulls and goats and the ashes of a heifer, sprinkling the unclean, sanctifies for the purifying of the flesh, ¹⁴ how much more shall the blood of Christ, who through the eternal Spirit offered Himself without spot to God, <u>cleanse your conscience</u> from dead works to serve the living God?

---

1. The author of Hebrews has been discussing the inadequacies of the old covenant, the old sanctuary, and the old priesthood. But now, he focuses on the new covenant that Jesus has brought. The rituals in the Old Testament required the high priest to take the blood of a bull and the blood of a goat with him when he entered the inner sanctuary on the Day of Atonement. But with what did Jesus enter the heavenly sanctuary (see verses 11–12)?

His own blood

2. The Old Testament sacrifices achieved outward ceremonial purification for the individual. But what did the blood of Christ accomplish (see verses 13–14)?

The Mediator's Death Necessary (Hebrews 9:15–17)

> ¹⁵ And for this reason He is the Mediator of the new covenant, by means of death, for the redemption of the transgressions under the first covenant, that those who are called may receive the promise of the eternal inheritance. ¹⁶ For where there is a testament, there must also of necessity be the death of the testator. ¹⁷ For a testament is in force after men are dead, since it has no power at all while the testator lives.

3. The Lord had declared under the old covenant that a blood sacrifice was required for the atonement of sins. "For the life of the flesh is in the blood, and I have given it to you upon the altar to make atonement for your souls" (Leviticus 17:11). The same would be required under the new covenant. How was this requirement fulfilled (see Hebrews 9:15)?

4. The author makes a play on words in this passage that is lost in English. The Greek word translated "covenant" in verse 15 can also mean "will," as in "last will and testament." A will does not go into effect until the testator has died. How does this relate to Christ? How does this show we are now living under the new testament (see verses 16–17)?

Greatness of Christ's Sacrifice (Hebrews 9:18–24)

[18] Therefore not even the first covenant was dedicated without blood. [19] For when Moses had spoken every precept to all the people according to the law, he took the blood of calves and goats, with water, scarlet wool, and hyssop, and sprinkled both the book itself and all the people, [20] saying, "This is the blood of the covenant which God has commanded you."

[21] Then likewise he sprinkled with blood both the tabernacle and all the vessels of the ministry. [22] And according to the law almost all things are purified with blood, and without shedding of blood there is no remission.

[23] Therefore it was necessary that the copies of the things in the heavens should be purified with these, but the heavenly things themselves with better sacrifices than these. [24] For Christ has not

entered the holy places made with hands, which are copies of the true, but into heaven itself, now to appear in the presence of God for us . . .

---

5. The ceremony described in verses 18–20 is based on the account of Moses affirming the first covenant at Mount Sinai: "Moses took the blood, sprinkled it on the people, and said, 'This is the blood of the covenant which the Lord has made with you according to all these words'" (Exodus 24:8). Why was the shedding of blood necessary (see Hebrews 9:21–22)?

6. Everything under the old covenant served as "copies of the things in the heavens" (verse 23). A copy is patterned after the original, so the sacrifices made under the old covenant were inferior to what was to come under the new. Why is the sacrifice that Jesus made better in this regard? What has Christ done for us through His sacrifice that none of the Old Testament priests could do (see verses 23–24)?

THE GREAT MEDIATOR

Christ Was Offered to Bear the Sins of Many (Hebrews 9:25–28)

²⁵ . . . not that He should offer Himself often, as the high priest enters the Most Holy Place every year with blood of another—²⁶ He then would have had to suffer often since the foundation of the world; but now, once at the end of the ages, He has appeared to put away sin by the sacrifice of Himself. ²⁷ And as it is appointed for men to die once, but after this the judgment, ²⁸ so Christ was offered once to bear the sins of many. To those who eagerly wait for Him He will appear a second time, apart from sin, for salvation.

7. The Day of Atonement ritual, which was performed every year, is now contrasted with Jesus' sacrifice on the cross. What was different about the sacrifice that Jesus made as compared to the former system (see verses 25–26)?

8. The author emphasizes the once-and-for-all nature of Jesus' sacrifice by comparing it to the human experience of death. Just as we die once and are subject to judgment, so the sacrifice that provides salvation from that judgment was needed only once. Jesus came into the world to bear our sins and serve as our perfect sacrifice. What is the promise now for those who accept this sacrifice made on their behalf (see verses 27–28)?

Reviewing the Story

The earthly tabernacle and old covenant were merely copies of the heavenly tabernacle and new covenant that were to come. Under the old covenant, a blood sacrifice was required to atone for people's sins. This requirement went back to the very beginning when God first established His covenant with the Israelites at Mount Sinai. But the priests could offer only temporary mediation under this system. The blood of the bulls and goats they carried into God's presence covered the people's sins only for a year. But Jesus entered into God's presence—the "heavenly sanctuary"—with the blood of His own sacrifice. He is the great Mediator who has restored our relationship with God forever.

9. What did Jesus obtain for us through His own blood (see Hebrews 9:12)? *eternal redemption*

THE GREAT MEDIATOR

10. How did Jesus become our mediator before God (see Hebrews 9:15)?

11. Why did the new covenant have to be dedicated with blood (see Hebrews 9:22)?

12. What is the promise for those who accept Christ's sacrifice (see Hebrews 9:27–28)?

Applying the Message

13. How do you respond to the truth that Jesus is right now serving as your intercessor and mediator before God?

14. How will you express your gratitude for the perfect sacrifice Jesus made on your behalf?

Reflecting on the Meaning

In this section of Hebrews, the author continues to point out to his readers that the new covenant is superior to anything the old covenant had to offer. In fact, the old covenant was merely an *inferior copy* of the greater heavenly covenant that was to come. As we examine this new covenant, four key principles stand out as to why it is better than the old covenant.

First, Jesus has provided a better righteousness. "Therefore it was necessary that the copies of the things in the heavens should be purified with these, but the heavenly things themselves with better sacrifices than these" (Hebrews 9:23). The sacrifices under the old covenant could not provide true holiness before God. As a result, because of our sin, God could never be fully satisfied with us. But He is satisfied with His own Son. And because of Jesus' mediating sacrifice for us, we now stand before the Father in the righteousness of the Son.

Second, Jesus has provided a better representation. "For Christ has not entered the holy places made with hands . . . but into heaven itself, now to appear in the presence of God for us" (verse 24). Jesus is not only our mediator but also our advocate and our defense attorney. He has entered into the presence of God on our behalf to represent us before the Father.

Third, Jesus has provided a better remission. "Not that He should offer Himself often . . . He then would have had to suffer often since the foundation of the world; but now, once at the end of the ages, He has appeared to put away sin by the sacrifice of Himself" (verses 25–26). Jesus is making intercession for us daily, but He is not being sacrificed for us daily. His sacrifice was once for all, and it never needs to be repeated. Just as man only dies once, Christ dealt with sin one time through His death. The problem of sin has been dealt with forever.

Fourth, Jesus has provided a better return. "To those who eagerly wait for Him He will appear a second time, apart from sin, for salvation" (verse 28). On the Day of Atonement, the high priest would disappear into the Most Holy Place with the blood of atonement to make intercession for the people. Outside, the people would wait to see if he had survived his dangerous assignment and his offering had been accepted. Jesus also passed from sight after His death and resurrection and ascended into heaven to intercede for us. But we do not have to wonder if His sacrifice will be accepted. We have the promise of Scripture that our High Priest *will* appear a second time to receive those who are eagerly waiting for Him.

If the appearance of the old covenant high priest was met with such glory and majesty, just imagine what it will be like when our High Priest, our Savior, returns in glory!

Journaling Your Response

How does your life reflect the fact that you are *eagerly* awaiting the return of Jesus?

LESSON *nine*

FAITH, HOPE, AND LOVE
Hebrews 10:1–39

Getting Started

How have the believers in your community of faith helped you in your walk with the Lord?

Setting the Stage

An unsettled conscience is a dangerous companion. Guilt and shame can drive us to do irrational things. The need to atone for our wrongdoing is hardwired into our makeup. We need forgiveness. We need to know that our sins do not define us in God's eyes.

The sacrificial system under the old covenant offered a temporary fix to the problem. God had instructed that atonement for sins could be secured through the spilling of an animal's blood—oxen, cattle, sheep, goats, doves, or pigeons. But the sheer numbers of sacrifices required spoke to the ineffectiveness of the system. It has been estimated that for a single Passover feast, more than 300,000 lambs were killed. For a person who lived to age sixty-seven, close to 116,000 sacrifices were required over his or her lifetime.

The author of Hebrews did not need these statistics to draw his conclusion. If the old system had been able to purge people of sin, not more than one sacrifice would have been needed. All the sacrifices really accomplished was to make those who offered them more aware of their sinful selves. The repetitive nature of the sacrifices created a consciousness of sin, not a cleansing from it. Even more burdensome was the reality that the sacrifices reminded people that God remembered their sin and the wayward direction of their hearts.

In this chapter of Hebrews, the writer identifies what God *truly* desires instead of animal sacrifices. Using passages from Psalms and Jeremiah, he shows how the wholehearted obedience of God's Son, and the perfect sacrifice that resulted from it, accomplished what millions and millions of animal sacrifices could not. He reassures us that Jesus' work on our behalf makes us perfect in God's eyes. His sacrifice is the source of our faith, hope, and love.

Exploring the Text

Animal Sacrifices Insufficient (Hebrews 10:1–10)

> ¹ For the law, having a shadow of the good things to come, and not the very image of the things, can never with these same sacrifices, which they offer continually year by year, make those who approach perfect. ² For then would they not have ceased to be offered? For the worshipers, once purified, would have had no more consciousness of sins. ³ But in those sacrifices there is a reminder of sins every year. ⁴ For it is not possible that the blood of bulls and goats could take away sins.

⁵ Therefore, when He came into the world, He said:

"Sacrifice and offering You did not desire,
But a body You have prepared for Me.
⁶ In burnt offerings and sacrifices for sin
You had no pleasure.
⁷ Then I said, 'Behold, I have come—
In the volume of the book it is written of Me—
To do Your will, O God.' "

⁸ Previously saying, "Sacrifice and offering, burnt offerings, and offerings for sin You did not desire, nor had pleasure in them" (which are offered according to the law), ⁹ then He said, "Behold, I have come to do Your will, O God." He takes away the first that He may establish the second. ¹⁰ By that will we have been sanctified through the offering of the body of Jesus Christ once for all.

---

1. The author of Hebrews builds on his theme that the old covenant—with its earthly tabernacle, priesthood, sacrifices, and system of laws—was merely a "copy" or "shadow" of the greater covenant to come through Christ. He quotes David's words in Psalm 40:6–8 to remind his readers that he is not the first person to take this viewpoint. How did David describe God's attitude toward animal sacrifices (see verses 1–7)?

2. The Greek word translated "takes away" in verse 9 is more accurately translated as "remove" or "destroy." It was generally used to refer to a person being "removed" or killed. What would this have communicated to the author's Jewish-Christian audience as it relates to their temptation to return to their former ways under Judaism (see verses 8–10)?

_____

_____

_____

_____

_____

Christ's Death Perfects the Sanctified (Hebrews 10:11–18)

¹¹ And every priest stands ministering daily and offering repeatedly the same sacrifices, which can never take away sins. ¹² But this Man, after He had offered one sacrifice for sins forever, sat down at the right hand of God, ¹³ from that time waiting till His enemies are made His footstool. ¹⁴ For by one offering He has perfected forever those who are being sanctified.

¹⁵ But the Holy Spirit also witnesses to us; for after He had said before,

¹⁶ "This is the covenant that I will make with them after those days, says the Lord: I will put My laws into their hearts, and in their minds I will write them," ¹⁷ then He adds, "Their sins and their lawless deeds I will remember no more." ¹⁸ Now where there is remission of these, there is no longer an offering for sin.

---

3. The statement in verses 12–14 is drawn from Psalm 110:1 ("The Lord said to my Lord, 'Sit at My right hand, till I make Your enemies Your footstool'") to suggest a sense of completion that has now been attained through Jesus's work. How do these triumphant images convey a successful finishing of priestly tasks?

4. The reference back to Jeremiah 31:33–34 in verses 16–17 emphasizes the perfection and holiness that was achieved through Christ's sacrifice. What does God say in these verses about the "new covenant" that He is making with those who accept Jesus' sacrifice?

Hold Fast Your Confession (Hebrews 10:19–25)

¹⁹ Therefore, brethren, having boldness to enter the Holiest by the blood of Jesus, ²⁰ by a new and living way which He consecrated for us, through the veil, that is, His flesh, ²¹ and having a High Priest over the house of God, ²² let us draw near with a true heart in full assurance of faith, having our hearts sprinkled from an evil conscience and our bodies washed with pure water. ²³ Let us hold fast the confession of our hope without wavering, for He who promised is faithful. ²⁴ And

LETTER TO THE HEBREWS

let us consider one another in order to stir up love and good works, ²⁵ not forsaking the assembling of ourselves together, as is the manner of some, but exhorting one another, and so much the more as you see the Day approaching.

---

5. The word *therefore* used in verse 19 indicates that the principles just discussed will now be related to the lives of believers in Christ. What can we now do "boldly" that followers of God could not do under the old system? What is the "assurance of faith" that we now have because of the way that Jesus has made for us (see verses 19–22)?

6. As we have seen, some of the recipients of Hebrews were questioning whether it was worth it to follow after Christ and were influencing others in the community to question the same. What instruction is given for the readers to fight back against this attitude? What is the importance of them continuing to assemble together (see verses 23–25)?

The Just Live by Faith (Hebrews 10:26–39)

²⁶ For if we sin willfully after we have received the knowledge of the truth, there no longer remains a sacrifice for sins, ²⁷ but a certain fearful expectation of judgment, and fiery indignation which will devour the adversaries. ²⁸ Anyone who has rejected Moses' law dies without mercy on the testimony of two or three witnesses. ²⁹ Of how much worse punishment, do you suppose, will he be thought worthy who has trampled the Son of God underfoot, counted the blood of the covenant by which he was sanctified a common thing, and insulted the Spirit of grace? ³⁰ For we know Him who said, "Vengeance is Mine, I will repay," says the Lord. And again, "The Lord will judge His people." ³¹ It is a fearful thing to fall into the hands of the living God.

³² But recall the former days in which, after you were illuminated, you endured a great struggle with sufferings: ³³ partly while you were made a spectacle both by reproaches and tribulations, and partly while you became companions of those who were so treated; ³⁴ for you had compassion on me in my chains, and joyfully accepted the plundering of your goods, knowing that you have a better and an enduring possession for yourselves in heaven. ³⁵ Therefore do not cast away your confidence, which has great reward. ³⁶ For you have need of endurance, so that after you have done the will of God, you may receive the promise:

> ³⁷ "For yet a little while,
> And He who is coming will come and will not tarry.
> ³⁸ Now the just shall live by faith;
> But if anyone draws back,
> My soul has no pleasure in him."

³⁹ But we are not of those who draw back to perdition, but of those who believe to the saving of the soul.

7. The writer of Hebrews has now stressed the benefits that believers in Christ receive under the new covenant. But he cannot leave this discussion without a warning of the *consequences* for those who choose not to heed his words. Of what various offenses are people guilty if they decide to reject the loving sacrifice of Christ (see verses 26–31)?

8. The exhortation to "recall the former days" is a call for the readers to stand firm in their faith and exhibit the faithfulness they have already displayed. When they first came to Christ, they endured sufferings, reproaches, and tribulations, but they continued to model Jesus to the world through their actions and deeds. Now they need to *endure*. What promise do they have that it will be worth it (see verses 32–39)?

Reviewing the Story

In this chapter of Hebrews, the author begins to apply the principles that he has discussed in previous chapters to our walk with Christ. Since Christ's death takes away our sins completely—something the animal sacrifices of the old covenant could never accomplish—we have access to the very presence of God. We can be bold in approaching the throne of our heavenly Father. We can also be confident in our faith and hold fast to it. As we stand with our brothers and sisters in Christ, we can be certain that our perseverance will one day be rewarded.

9. What did Jesus' once-for-all sacrifice accomplish for us (see Hebrews 10:10)?

10. How does our relationship with God change because of Jesus' sacrifice (see Hebrews 10:16–17)?

11. How should our new standing before God impact the way we interact with others (see Hebrews 10:19–24)?

LETTER TO THE HEBREWS

12. What should we do when our confidence starts to waver and our endurance starts to flag (see Hebrews 10:35–38)?

Applying the Message

13. How has the Lord worked through your struggles to make you stronger in your faith?

14. What are some of the sacrifices you have made to have compassion for others?

Reflecting on the Meaning

As the author of Hebrews writes this chapter, he turns from doctrine to duty, from creed to conduct, and from belief to behavior. He begins to explain how we are to respond to what we have already learned, especially as it concerns Jesus' role as our forerunner. Since Christ has ascended and is at the right hand of the Father, He is our heavenly high priest, assuring us we have not only access to God but also an advocate before Him. Based on that understanding, there are three things we must do to experience all that God has for us through Christ Jesus.

First, we must draw near to God. "Let us draw near with a true heart in full assurance of faith" (Hebrews 10:22). Because of Christ, we are now invited to approach God's throne, with confidence, and receive mercy and grace through Jesus Christ. Our "full assurance of faith" is a confession on our part that we believe God has forgiven us and will keep His promises to us. This is faith! We come before God with confidence instead of doubting.

Second, we must hold fast in hope. "Let us hold fast the confession of our hope without wavering, for He who promised is faithful" (verse 23). Our hope for the future is based on the promises of Almighty God. We can hold fast because He has promised to be faithful to us. And because His faithfulness never wavers, our hope can never be extinguished. There is no reason for it to change with our circumstances. We can remain positive when situations seem to call for negativity by looking at the big picture of our hope.

Third, we reach out in love. "And let us consider one another in order to stir up love and good works . . . exhorting one another, and so much the more as you see the Day approaching" (verses 24–25). The word *consider* speaks of concentrated thought and focus. We are not to take one another for granted but rather to take note of each other. We are to be conscious of the influence we can have on each other. We are to "stir up love and good works."

God has drawn near to us so that we may draw near to Him. He has given us His hope as an anchor for our souls. Now, we are able to reach out to others with that same hope. As we do, we experience all that God has to offer us and change lives in the process.

Journaling Your Response

What are some practical acts of "love and good works" that you can do for someone today?

LESSON *ten*

THE POWER OF FAITH
Hebrews 11:1–40

Getting Started

What is your personal definition of "faith"?

Setting the Stage

The heroes of the Bible stand out because of their perseverance in trusting God in the midst of challenging circumstances. Noah's faith allowed him to build the ark in the midst of an unrighteous generation. Abraham's faith led him to leave his people and travel to an unknown land in response to God's call. Isaac's faith led him to willingly offer himself on the altar. David's faith propelled him to confront the giant Goliath. Elijah's faith led him propose a showdown between himself and the 400 prophets of Baal. Daniel's faith led him to defy a king's edict rather than stop praying each day to his Lord. And if you remain true to the cause of Christ, there will be times when your faith will lead you take risks of your own.

One of the unmistakable messages from this next chapter of Hebrews is that perseverance and bold action is required when pursuing God's call on our lives. Sometimes, this will mean that we will be going against the prevailing wisdom of our culture. Certainly, God created us to enjoy fellowship and get along with people, but there will be times when we will have to step out and make choices that are unpopular and even baffling to others. God will call us at times to put aside distractions, refuse to be swayed by outside influences, and fight against our need for other people's approval—all of which can play havoc with our mission.

It is no coincidence that most, if not all, of the people mentioned in the "Faith Hall of Fame" of Hebrews 11 experienced times when they were isolated and scorned because of their decision to boldly follow God. Standing alone takes us out of our comfort zone and away from the safety of the crowd. It forces us to look only to God for what we need. It stretches and strengthens our faith in Him. And, as read in Hebrews 11, we have an everlasting testimony of what faith, forged in the crucible of aloneness, can accomplish in our lives.

EXPLORING THE TEXT

By Faith (Hebrews 11:1–7)

> [1] Now faith is the substance of things hoped for, the evidence of things not seen. [2] For by it the elders obtained a good testimony.

³ By faith we understand that the worlds were framed by the word of God, so that the things which are seen were not made of things which are visible.

⁴ By faith Abel offered to God a more excellent sacrifice than Cain, through which he obtained witness that he was righteous, God testifying of his gifts; and through it he being dead still speaks.

⁵ By faith Enoch was taken away so that he did not see death, "and was not found, because God had taken him"; for before he was taken he had this testimony, that he pleased God. ⁶ But without faith it is impossible to please Him, for he who comes to God must believe that He is, and that He is a rewarder of those who diligently seek Him.

⁷ By faith Noah, being divinely warned of things not yet seen, moved with godly fear, prepared an ark for the saving of his household, by which he condemned the world and became heir of the righteousness which is according to faith.

---

1. The author of Hebrews opens with a declaration of what faith is. This statement will serve as the foundation for the examples from Scripture that he will go on to cite. He notes that the life of faith involves *looking forward* to the fulfillment of God's promises and *looking up* to the unseen reality of God's presence. How does this explanation apply to the Jewish Christians who were experiencing doubt (see verses 1–3)?

_____
_____
_____
_____
_____
_____
_____
_____

LETTER TO THE HEBREWS

2. How did Abel, Enoch, and Noah all display faith? How did Enoch please God? What is required to build such a relationship (see verses 4–7)?

_____

_____

_____

_____

_____

The Heavenly Hope (Hebrews 11:8–20)

⁸ By faith Abraham obeyed when he was called to go out to the place which he would receive as an inheritance. And he went out, not knowing where he was going. ⁹ By faith he dwelt in the land of promise as in a foreign country, dwelling in tents with Isaac and Jacob, the heirs with him of the same promise; ¹⁰ for he waited for the city which has foundations, whose builder and maker is God.

¹¹ By faith Sarah herself also received strength to conceive seed, and she bore a child when she was past the age, because she judged Him faithful who had promised. ¹² Therefore from one man, and him as good as dead, were born as many as the stars of the sky in multitude—innumerable as the sand which is by the seashore.

¹³ These all died in faith, not having received the promises, but having seen them afar off were assured of them, embraced them and confessed that they were strangers and pilgrims on the earth. ¹⁴ For those who say such things declare plainly that they seek a homeland. ¹⁵ And truly if they had called to mind that country from which they had come out, they would have had opportunity to return. ¹⁶ But now they desire a better, that is, a heavenly country. Therefore God is not ashamed to be called their God, for He has prepared a city for them.

¹⁷ By faith Abraham, when he was tested, offered up Isaac, and he who had received the promises offered up his only begotten

son, ¹⁸ of whom it was said, "In Isaac your seed shall be called," ¹⁹ concluding that God was able to raise him up, even from the dead, from which he also received him in a figurative sense.

²⁰ By faith Isaac blessed Jacob and Esau concerning things to come.

---

3. How did Abraham, Sarah, and Isaac exhibit faith in God? How were they and the others "pilgrims" on this earth (see verses 8–14, 17–20)?

4. God was so entwined with the family history of the Old Testament patriarchs that He allowed Himself to be identified as "the God of Abraham, the God of Isaac, and the God of Jacob" (Exodus 3:6, 15–16; 4:5; Matthew 22:32; Mark 12:26; Luke 20:37; Acts 7:32). Their story ended with them still waiting for the fulfillment of God's promises. What does God have in store for them (see Hebrews 11:15–16)?

The Faith of the Patriarchs (Hebrews 11:21–29)

²¹ By faith Jacob, when he was dying, blessed each of the sons of Joseph, and worshiped, leaning on the top of his staff.

²² By faith Joseph, when he was dying, made mention of the departure of the children of Israel, and gave instructions concerning his bones.

²³ By faith Moses, when he was born, was hidden three months by his parents, because they saw he was a beautiful child; and they were not afraid of the king's command.

²⁴ By faith Moses, when he became of age, refused to be called the son of Pharaoh's daughter, ²⁵ choosing rather to suffer affliction with the people of God than to enjoy the passing pleasures of sin, ²⁶ esteeming the reproach of Christ greater riches than the treasures in Egypt; for he looked to the reward.

²⁷ By faith he forsook Egypt, not fearing the wrath of the king; for he endured as seeing Him who is invisible. ²⁸ By faith he kept the Passover and the sprinkling of blood, lest he who destroyed the firstborn should touch them.

²⁹ By faith they passed through the Red Sea as by dry land, whereas the Egyptians, attempting to do so, were drowned.

5. How did Jacob, Joseph, and Moses demonstrate faith in God? What did Moses—who put ultimate realities ahead of his present advantages—forfeit in order to belong to the people of God (see verses 21–29)?

THE POWER OF FAITH

6. The author's words in verses 24–26 represent the "substance of things hoped for" perspective of faith that he mentioned back in verse 1. How does this statement in verse 27 represent the "evidence of things not seen" perspective of verse 1?

_____

_____

_____

_____

_____

_____

_____

By Faith They Overcame (Hebrews 11:30–40)

³⁰ By faith the walls of Jericho fell down after they were encircled for seven days. ³¹ By faith the harlot Rahab did not perish with those who did not believe, when she had received the spies with peace.

³² And what more shall I say? For the time would fail me to tell of Gideon and Barak and Samson and Jephthah, also of David and Samuel and the prophets: ³³ who through faith subdued kingdoms, worked righteousness, obtained promises, stopped the mouths of lions, ³⁴ quenched the violence of fire, escaped the edge of the sword, out of weakness were made strong, became valiant in battle, turned to flight the armies of the aliens. ³⁵ Women received their dead raised to life again.

Others were tortured, not accepting deliverance, that they might obtain a better resurrection. ³⁶ Still others had trial of mockings and scourgings, yes, and of chains and imprisonment. ³⁷ They were stoned, they were sawn in two, were tempted, were slain with the sword. They wandered about in sheepskins and goatskins, being destitute, afflicted, tormented—³⁸ of whom the world was not worthy. They wandered in deserts and mountains, in dens and caves of the earth.

³⁹ And all these, having obtained a good testimony through faith, did not receive the promise, ⁴⁰ God having provided something better for us, that they should not be made perfect apart from us.

---

7. How did Rahab and the Israelites entering the Promised Land show faith? What were the results? What were some of the outcomes of the faith that others like Gideon, Barak, Samson, Jephthah, David, and Samuel displayed (see verses 32–35)?

8. The rapid-fire list that concludes the chapter may be divided into two categories: (1) success stories of people who experienced God's deliverance (see verses 33–35a), and (2) stark reminders of the price of following God (see verses 35b–38). What did those who paid the ultimate price for their faith receive in return (see verses 33–38)?

Reviewing the Story

The author of Hebrews reminds his readers of the faith exhibited by their ancestors. He begins with the sacrifice offered by Abel, notes especially the faith of Abraham and Moses, and continues selectively down to the main figures involved in the conquest of the Promised Land under Joshua. He packs the remaining twelve centuries of Jewish history into a short summary—mentioning even those who suffered and died for their faith—but leaves no doubt their faith was rewarded.

9. How did the people of God who lived before Jesus obtain "a good testimony" in God's eyes (see Hebrews 11:2)?

10. How did the people of faith treat the promises of God that they did not get to see fulfilled (see Hebrews 11:13)?

11. What were God's people willing to endure for their faith (see Hebrews 11:35)?

12. What was the difference between the faith of the Old Testament heroes and that of the Jewish Christians to whom Hebrews was written (see Hebrews 11:39–40)?

Applying the Message

13. Why is it important to remember the faith of those who have gone before you?

14. What evidence of Hebrews 11 faith might people see in your life?

_____
_____
_____
_____

Reflecting on the Meaning

One takeaway from this section of Hebrews is that true faith—the kind that people talk about centuries later—is not idle but extremely *active*.

Just look at the individuals the author of Hebrews selects as examples of the faith. Abel *brings* the proper sacrifice. Enoch *walks* with God. Noah *builds* an ark. Abraham *embarks* on a journey, *dwells* in tents in a foreign country, and *looks* for a city whose builder and maker is God. Sarah *bears* a child past the age of childbearing. Abraham *offers* up that child in obedience as a sacrifice to God, *believing* that God can raise his son from the dead.

As the story moves to the land of Egypt, Moses *refuses* to be called the son of Pharaoh's daughter, *chooses* to suffer affliction with the people of God, and *esteems* God's riches to be greater than the treasures of Egypt. The Israelites *forsake* Egypt for the Promised Land and *walk* through the Red Sea as on dry ground. Centuries later, when they finally arrive, the faithful sons and daughters of God *walk* around Jericho until the walls fall down.

The faithful of God go on to *subdue* kingdoms, *work* righteousness, *obtain* promises, *stop* the mouths of lions, *quench* the violence of fire, *escape* the edge of the sword, and *defeat* enemies. Some *endure* torture, mockings, scourgings, and chains. Others are willing to even *face* stonings and death at the hands of executioners. But all *act* and step out in faith.

The same must be true of us. If we profess that we believe in God, we must *act* upon that confession of faith. In return, God promises that if we place our faith in His Son alone for eternal life, He will give us His Son as our Savior. We will spend eternity with Him in a place that is being prepared for all those who also choose to trust in Him.

Journaling Your Response

How do you exhibit this kind of *active* faith in Christ?

LESSON *eleven*

RUNNING WITH ENDURANCE

Hebrews 12:1–29

Getting Started

What are some things that help you endure—to finish something no matter how long it takes?

Setting the Stage

The author of Hebrews has just concluded his dialogue on notable characters in Jewish history who stand out from the rest because of their faith. His concluding remarks shifted the conversation from a past-day exploration of historical events to a present-day application for his readers. As he wrote, "All these, having obtained a good testimony through faith, did not receive the promise, God having provided something better for us" (11:39–40).

The writer wanted his readers to understand they were a part of this greater journey of faith that had begun long ago with their ancestors. It was as if they had all joined the same "race." As is the case with all races, running it effectively requires great discipline and endurance—especially in the face of persecution. Many of his readers were certainly enduring such suffering and were considering ending the race prematurely. But he wanted them to know that those who had gone before them—their heroes like Moses, Abraham, and David—were watching from the sidelines and cheering them on. They needed to reach the finish line.

The author's motivating message can be summarized in three words: "looking unto Jesus" (verse 2). Jesus is the "author" of our faith—the one who has blazed the trail. He has already run this race, so He knows how to proceed. He stays a pace or two ahead of us all the way to the finish line. He shows us where the obstacles are and directs each step we take. But He is also the "finisher" of our faith. He has already completed the course and reached the end successfully. He claimed victory after enduring unimaginable suffering, hostility, and disgrace.

So, when we consider Jesus, we realize that our challenges pale in comparison. He has seen it all, experienced it all, and triumphed over it all. Through His strength, we can be victorious as well. We just need to keep our eyes completely fixed on Him as we run.

Exploring the Text

The Race of Faith (Hebrews 12:1–11)

¹ Therefore we also, since we are surrounded by so great a cloud of witnesses, let us lay aside every weight, and the sin which so easily ensnares us, and let us run with endurance the race that is set before

us, ²looking unto Jesus, the author and finisher of our faith, who for the joy that was set before Him endured the cross, despising the shame, and has sat down at the right hand of the throne of God.

³ For consider Him who endured such hostility from sinners against Himself, lest you become weary and discouraged in your souls. ⁴ You have not yet resisted to bloodshed, striving against sin. ⁵ And you have forgotten the exhortation which speaks to you as to sons:

> "My son, do not despise the chastening of the LORD,
> Nor be discouraged when you are rebuked by Him;
> ⁶ For whom the LORD loves He chastens,
> And scourges every son whom He receives."

⁷ If you endure chastening, God deals with you as with sons; for what son is there whom a father does not chasten? ⁸ But if you are without chastening, of which all have become partakers, then you are illegitimate and not sons.

⁹ Furthermore, we have had human fathers who corrected us, and we paid them respect. Shall we not much more readily be in subjection to the Father of spirits and live? ¹⁰ For they indeed for a few days chastened us as seemed best to them, but He for our profit, that we may be partakers of His holiness. ¹¹ Now no chastening seems to be joyful for the present, but painful; nevertheless, afterward it yields the peaceable fruit of righteousness to those who have been trained by it.

---

1. The use of the word *therefore* indicates that we are again coming to a point of application in Hebrews. All of the heroes of the faith that have been mentioned in the previous chapter are surrounding us like "a cloud of witnesses." But the focus is not to be on them but on "looking unto Jesus." The Greek word for this particular phrase is found nowhere else in the New Testament. It means to "look away from everything else and to fix one's eyes trustingly." Why does Jesus deserve this solitary focus (see verses 1–3)?

_____
_____
_____
_____
_____
_____

2. Our encouragement is to endure in our faith by keeping our focus solely on Christ—our model for persevering in the midst of hostility. Furthermore, we are to accept God's discipline in our struggle. The words quoted in verses 5–6 are from Proverbs 3:11–12, which are written as from a father to his son. How are we to respond to God's discipline? What is the reason for this discipline in our lives (see verses 4–11)?

_____
_____
_____
_____
_____
_____

Renew Your Spiritual Vitality (Hebrews 12:12–17)

¹² Therefore strengthen the hands which hang down, and the feeble knees, ¹³ and make straight paths for your feet, so that what is lame may not be dislocated, but rather be healed.

¹⁴ Pursue peace with all people, and holiness, without which no one will see the Lord: ¹⁵ looking carefully lest anyone fall short of the grace of God; lest any root of bitterness springing up cause trouble,

RUNNING WITH ENDURANCE

and by this many become defiled; ¹⁶ lest there be any fornicator or profane person like Esau, who for one morsel of food sold his birthright. ¹⁷ For you know that afterward, when he wanted to inherit the blessing, he was rejected, for he found no place for repentance, though he sought it diligently with tears.

3. The author's instruction to "strengthen the hands . . . and the feeble knees" recalls his opening metaphor of a runner who, as the race progresses, is now running out of strength. How does this relate to the situation that he believed his audience was facing? What does he instruct his readers to do to remedy this problem (see verses 12–14)?

4. Esau, who is cited in verse 16, was willing to give up his inheritance for a single meal (see Genesis 25:29–34). What is the message to Christians who might be tempted to give up their heavenly calling in exchange for some temporary relief (see verses 15–17)?

The Glorious Company (Hebrews 12:18–24)

¹⁸ For you have not come to the mountain that may be touched and that burned with fire, and to blackness and darkness and tempest, ¹⁹ and the sound of a trumpet and the voice of words, so that those who heard it begged that the word should not be spoken to them anymore. ²⁰ (For they could not endure what was commanded: "And if so much as a beast touches the mountain, it shall be stoned or shot with an arrow." ²¹ And so terrifying was the sight that Moses said, "I am exceedingly afraid and trembling.")

²² But you have come to Mount Zion and to the city of the living God, the heavenly Jerusalem, to an innumerable company of angels, ²³ to the general assembly and church of the firstborn who are registered in heaven, to God the Judge of all, to the spirits of just men made perfect, ²⁴ to Jesus the Mediator of the new covenant, and to the blood of sprinkling that speaks better things than that of Abel.

---

5. The image of the mountain in verses 18–21 is drawn from the Israelites' experience at Mount Sinai, as depicted in Exodus 19–20, where God established the old covenant with His people. How does this passage in Hebrews describe the way in which that covenant was given? What does this suggest about the limitations of the old covenant?

6. The old covenant at Mount Sinai required the people to be kept separate from a fearsome and holy God. The second covenant, given at the heavenly Mount Zion, removed that barrier. How does the author describe these differences? What kind of citizenship are given to those who choose to be part of the new covenant (see verses 22–24)?

_____

_____

_____

_____

_____

_____

Hear the Heavenly Voice (Hebrews 12:25–29)

[25] See that you do not refuse Him who speaks. For if they did not escape who refused Him who spoke on earth, much more shall we not escape if we turn away from Him who speaks from heaven, [26] whose voice then shook the earth; but now He has promised, saying, "Yet once more I shake not only the earth, but also heaven." [27] Now this, "Yet once more," indicates the removal of those things that are being shaken, as of things that are made, that the things which cannot be shaken may remain.

[28] Therefore, since we are receiving a kingdom which cannot be shaken, let us have grace, by which we may serve God acceptably with reverence and godly fear. [29] For our God is a consuming fire.

7. The writer of Hebrews frequently alternates between encouraging his readers to persevere in their faith and warning them of the consequences for failing to do so. Here, he returns to his method of offering a warning for those who choose not to accept his counsel. What does he remind his readers about the God whom they serve—the same God who once appeared to the Israelites at Mount Sinai (see verses 25–26)?

---

8. The author previously spoke of the thunder, lightning, thick clouds, and sound of trumpets that accompanied God giving the first covenant at Mount Sinai. Now, he adds that an earthquake shook the mountain at that time. Yet as fearful as that "shaking" might have been, it will be nothing compared to what will occur in the last days. What is the warning here for believers? How can one escape this great "shaking" (see verses 27–29)?

Reviewing the Story

The author of Hebrews draws on the imagery of a marathon to emphasize the need for all believers in Christ to persevere in running the race that has been set before them. He reminds us that we are not alone in this race—the very heroes of the faith that he has just described are standing on the sidelines and cheering us on. We need only fix our eyes on Jesus as we run and accept the discipline that God provides as a son accepts discipline from a loving father. The author then offers a warning to not give up our inheritance in Christ. We are to remember that we serve an awesome

God—the same One who struck fear into the Israelites' hearts when He appeared to them at Mount Sinai. We belong to an eternal kingdom that cannot be shaken. We must thus serve God with reverence and godly fear.

9. What is the best way to deal with God's discipline and chastening as we run the race that has been set before us (see Hebrews 12:5–8)?

10. What should be our attitude toward our fellow believers who are also running the races set before them (see Hebrews 12:14–17)?

11. What is the difference between the way we approach God under the new covenant and the way the Israelites approached Him under the old covenant (see Hebrews 12:18–24)?

12. How are believers in Christ to serve God (see Hebrews 12:28–29)?

Applying the Message

13. Why is it so important to keep your focus on Christ as you run the race that God has set before you? How do you manage to keep your gaze on Him in the midst of distractions?

14. How do you respond to the truth that God chastens those He loves? What are some ways that you have experienced His discipline lately in your life?

Reflecting on the Meaning

The author of Hebrews draws on the imagery of a runner in this chapter to show the kind of perseverance and endurance that will be required on our part to successfully follow Christ. This will be no light jog or easy morning run—and will be further complicated by the fact that we won't necessarily know the twists and turns along the way. We won't always know how rugged the road will be or even how far we will have to travel until we reach the end. But what we do have are three running strategies from Hebrews 12:1 that will help us along the way.

First, we must lay aside the things that encumber us. Some things in life weigh us down and keep us from running effectively. These things are not necessarily bad, but they can hinder our progress. For the Jewish-Christian recipients of Hebrews, that extra weight was their continued fascination with Judaism. For us, it may be such seemingly harmless things such as our need for comfort, security in our present situation, overindulgence in entertainment, or ambition to make money. There are many things we have to set aside if we are going to experience all that God has for us.

Second, we must lay aside the things that ensnare us. While the "extra things" in our lives might encumber us, the evil things will actually ensnare us. Sin has a way of taking us down and reducing our effectiveness for Christ. If we want to prevent this from happening, we must remember that at the root of this ensnaring is *unbelief*—our deliberate choice to not trust in God. In the Bible, we find that such unbelief came with great consequences. Unbelief cost the Israelites the loss of an entire generation. Unbelief caused Peter to begin sinking when he looked away from Jesus. We must reject this kind of unbelief and instead choose to accept God's truth.

Finally, we must lay aside the things that entangle us. In racing terms, this means staying in our own lane. God has called each of us to run the race that is "set before *us*." This means that we must focus on the tasks and priorities that He has given to us—and not worry about what anyone else is doing in their race. As we do this—relying on Christ as our source of strength—we will be able to effectively run the race that He has established for us.

Journaling Your Response

What do you need to lay aside as you run the race that is set before you?

LESSON *twelve*

THE SUPERIOR LIFE IN CHRIST

Hebrews 13:1–25

Getting Started

When was a time that you reached out to help someone even though you were in need? How did this help to shift the focus off the problem that you were facing?

Setting the Stage

When we face trials in this life, we can respond by either directing our focus *inward* or *outward*. An *inward* focus will lead to us dwelling on the misery and unfairness of it all. The result will be self-pity, doubt, and discontent. We will question why God allows bad things to happen to us when others seem to have it so good. An *outward* focus will lead us to recognize that others are struggling as well. We will turn our attention away from ourselves and toward them. We will recognize that our struggles have made us uniquely qualified to empathize with them.

The writer of Hebrews recognized that his Jewish-Christian readers had arrived at this place in their lives. They were enduring great persecution and were losing the strength to run their race. What they needed to do now was maintain an *outward* perspective on their struggles. They needed to realize that they were not alone—that others were suffering right along with them and needed their encouragement, support and strength.

In this final chapter of Hebrews, the advice takes the form of a series of rapid-fire exhortations that, at first glance, seem to have little connection with each other. However, a closer look reveals that all these exhortations focus on the opportunities the believers had to honor Christ. Up to this point, the case has been made for Jesus' greatness, showing He is superior to the prophets, angels, men like Moses and Joshua, the old covenant, and the Levitical priesthood. Now it was time for the believers to embrace this truth, come together as one, persevere in their race, and help their brothers and sisters in Christ who were stumbling.

We each, likewise, have the opportunity to reflect the greatness of our High Priest in the way that we respond to our trials. We can choose to turn *outward* and focus on others. We can determine to allow our common struggles to unite us and help us to persevere. We can embrace a spirit of sacrificial service and truly love one another.

Exploring the Text

Concluding Directives on Conduct (Hebrews 13:1–6)

> ¹ Let brotherly love continue. ² Do not forget to entertain strangers, for by so doing some have unwittingly entertained angels.

³ Remember the prisoners as if chained with them—those who are mistreated—since you yourselves are in the body also.

⁴ Marriage is honorable among all, and the bed undefiled; but fornicators and adulterers God will judge.

⁵ Let your conduct be without covetousness; be content with such things as you have. For He Himself has said, "I will never leave you nor forsake you." ⁶ So we may boldly say:

"The Lord is my helper;
I will not fear.
What can man do to me?"

---

1. The author of Hebrews has concluded his arguments for the superiority of Christ over the old covenant system. He now closes with some personal remarks, exhortations, encouragements, requests for prayer, and blessings. He begins with the statement to "let brotherly love continue." The word translated *love* is *philadelphia*, which emphasizes the bond between believers. What is our special responsibility to each other as fellow members of the family of God (see verses 1–4)?

2. The recognition is that covetousness will cause the believers to pursue an inward focus—a concentration on their desires instead of on the needs of others. What are the reasons as to why believers in Christ can be content with what they have (see verses 5–6)?

Remembering Leaders and Sound Doctrine (Hebrews 13:7–9)

> ⁷ Remember those who rule over you, who have spoken the word of God to you, whose faith follow, considering the outcome of their conduct. ⁸ Jesus Christ is the same yesterday, today, and forever. ⁹ Do not be carried about with various and strange doctrines. For it is good that the heart be established by grace, not with foods which have not profited those who have been occupied with them.

3. The reference to "those who rule over you" likely refers to the founders of the church to whom Hebrews was written. What were the believers to remember about these leaders (see verse 7)?

4. The readers were to remember the truth about Jesus that they had been taught. But what were they to reject (see verses 8–9)?

A Different Altar (Hebrews 13:10–16)

¹⁰ We have an altar from which those who serve the tabernacle have no right to eat. ¹¹ For the bodies of those animals, whose blood is brought into the sanctuary by the high priest for sin, are burned outside the camp. ¹² Therefore Jesus also, that He might sanctify the people with His own blood, suffered outside the gate. ¹³ Therefore let us go forth to Him, outside the camp, bearing His reproach. ¹⁴ For here we have no continuing city, but we seek the one to come. ¹⁵ Therefore by Him let us continually offer the sacrifice of praise to God, that is, the fruit of our lips, giving thanks to His name. ¹⁶ But do not forget to do good and to share, for with such sacrifices God is well pleased.

5. The imagery in this passage is of the Israelites gathering at the "altar" to offer sacrifices and feast together. What point is the writer making by stating that believers in Christ have an "altar" from which "those who serve the tabernacle" no longer have the right to eat (see verses 10–11)?

6. The author reminds us that Jesus was crucified outside the walls of the city. In Jewish terms, that meant "outside the camp," which signified being ostracized and excluded. How does this relate to his point that believers in Christ are no longer part of the old covenant? What is the instruction for believers to do as members of the new covenant (see verses 12–16?)

___

Final Exhortations and Benediction (Hebrews 13:17–25)

[17] Obey those who rule over you, and be submissive, for they watch out for your souls, as those who must give account. Let them do so with joy and not with grief, for that would be unprofitable for you.

[18] Pray for us; for we are confident that we have a good conscience, in all things desiring to live honorably. [19] But I especially urge you to do this, that I may be restored to you the sooner.

[20] Now may the God of peace who brought up our Lord Jesus from the dead, that great Shepherd of the sheep, through the blood of the everlasting covenant, [21] make you complete in every good work to do His will, working in you what is well pleasing in His sight, through Jesus Christ, to whom be glory forever and ever. Amen.

[22] And I appeal to you, brethren, bear with the word of exhortation, for I have written to you in few words. [23] Know that our brother Timothy has been set free, with whom I shall see you if he comes shortly.

[24] Greet all those who rule over you, and all the saints. Those from Italy greet you.

[25] Grace be with you all. Amen.

THE SUPERIOR LIFE IN CHRIST

7. The writer closes with a personal appeal for the believers to respect their Christian leaders and to pray for him. What is his specific request as it relates to honoring their godly leaders? What are his personal requests for their prayers (see verses 17–19)?

8. In the closing benediction or "blessing," the author draws on familiar imagery from the Gospels of Jesus as our Good Shepherd. How does he use this imagery to assure us that our resurrection is assured? What is his final appeal to his readers (see verses 20–25)?

Reviewing the Story

The writer of Hebrews concludes his letter with a series of exhortations. He instructs believers to love one another, show hospitality to all, remember those in prison, be faithful in marriage, and flee covetousness. He asks them to remember the example of their godly leaders and the doctrine they received. He reminds them that as members of the new covenant, they have nothing to do with the "altar" of their former ways under the old covenant. He implores them to honor their leaders, to submit to their authority, and to pray for him. He closes with a blessing, a prayer for continued growth, and final greetings for those in the church.

9. What are believers in Christ able to do, knowing that the Lord will never leave nor forsake us (see Hebrews 13:5–6)?

10. Why are we able to trust Christ (see Hebrews 13:8)?

11. What should be the attitude of those who serve in a leadership role (see Hebrews 13:17)?

12. What is the writer's prayer for his readers (see Hebrews 13:20–21)?

Applying the Message

13. What helps you to maintain an outward focus on others when you are going through trials?

14. How has this outward focus allowed you to empathize with others going through trials?

Reflecting on the Meaning

The author of Hebrews offers his closing benediction with these words: "Now may the God of peace . . . make you complete [or perfect] in every good work to do His will" (Hebrews 13:20–21). Earlier in the chapter, he identifies three areas of outward focus that are to be part of this perfecting work. The starting point for each can be summarized in the first four words of the chapter: "Let brotherly love continue" (verse 1).

First, we are to direct our love toward our fellow believers. The kind of love the author refers to in this verse is *"brotherly* love." This is a kind of love that suggests the members of the church had a responsibility to encourage, strengthen, support, and help one another persevere in the faith. Elsewhere, Paul suggests this love is a natural outgrowth of our decision to follow Christ: "But concerning brotherly love you have no need that I should write to you, for you yourselves are taught by God to love one another" (1 Thessalonians 4:9). Jesus Himself said, "By this all will know that you are My disciples, if you have love for one another" (John 13:35).

Second, we are to direct our love to those outside our group. The author of Hebrews instructs believers to "not forget to entertain strangers" (verse 2). In the early days of the church, when inns were scarce and usually unappealing, followers of Jesus opened their homes to fellow believers who were fleeing persecution, traveling as evangelists, or going from place to place on business. That same spirit of loving hospitality and concern should mark our interaction with those who are unknown to us.

Third, we are to direct our love to those who are forsaken. The author of Hebrews notes, "Remember the prisoners as if chained with them" (verse 3). At the time the letter was written, many followers of Christ were being imprisoned or singled out for persecution because of their faith. People in their community were reluctant to reach out to them, for fear of being identified with them and thereby placing a target on their own backs. The author of Hebrews wanted them to put this fear aside and embrace them as if they were in chains together.

As we direct our love toward our fellow believers, to those outside our group, and to the forsaken, we move from being *inner*-focused to *outer*-focused. We begin to share in other people's lives and discover, much to our surprise, that we are not alone in our struggles. We begin to truly fulfill Jesus' command to love our neighbors as ourselves (see Mark 12:31). And we reflect the light of God to a hurting world who desperately needs to experience His love.

Journaling Your Response

What is one practical way you will show the love of Christ to a hurting person this week?

LEADER'S GUIDE

Thank you for choosing to lead your group through this study from Dr. David Jeremiah on *The Letter to the Hebrews*. Being a group leader has its own rewards, and it is our prayer that your walk with the Lord will deepen through this experience. During the twelve lessons in this study, you and your group will read selected passages from these letters, explore key themes in them based on teachings from Dr. Jeremiah, and review questions that will encourage group discussion. There are multiple components in this section that can help you structure your lessons and discussion time, so please be sure to read and consider each one.

Before You Begin

Before your first meeting, make sure that you and your group are well-versed with the content of the lesson. Group members should have their own copy of *The Letter to the Hebrews Study Guide* to the first meeting so that they can follow along and record their answers, thoughts, and insights. After the first week, you may wish to assign the study guide lesson as homework prior to the group meeting and then use the meeting time to discuss the content in the lesson.

To ensure everyone has a chance to participate in the discussion, the ideal size for a group is around eight to ten people. If there are more than ten people, break up the bigger group into smaller subgroups. Make sure the members are committed to participating each week, as this will help create stability and help you better prepare the structure of the meeting.

At the beginning of each week's study, start with the opening Getting Started question to introduce the topic you will be discussing. The members should answer briefly, as the goal is just for them to have an idea of the subject in their minds as you go over the lesson. This will allow the members to become engaged and ready to interact with the rest of the group.

After reviewing the lesson, try to initiate a free-flowing discussion. Invite group members to bring questions and insights they may have discovered to the next meeting, especially if they were unsure of the meaning of some parts of the lesson. Be prepared to discuss how biblical truth applies to the world we live in today.

Weekly Preparation

As the group leader, here are a few things that you can do to prepare for each meeting:

- *Be thoroughly familiar with the material in the lesson.* Make sure that you understand the content of each lesson so you know how to structure the group time and are prepared to lead the group discussion.

- *Decide, ahead of time, which questions you want to discuss.* Depending on how much time you have each week, you may not be able to reflect on every question. Select specific questions that you feel will evoke the best discussion.

- *Take prayer requests.* At the end of your discussion, take prayer requests from your group members and then pray for one another.

Structuring the Discussion Time

There are several ways to structure the duration of the study. You can choose to cover each lesson individually, for a total of twelve weeks of group meetings, or you can combine two lessons together per week, for a total of six weeks of group meetings. The following charts illustrate these options:

TWELVE-WEEK FORMAT

Week	Lessons Covered	Reading
1	The Superiority of Christ	Hebrews 1:1–14
2	When God Became Man	Hebrews 2:1–18
3	A Soft Heart Toward God	Hebrews 3:1–19
4	Jesus Is All You Need	Hebrews 4:1–5:14
5	The Anchor of Hope	Hebrews 6:1–20
6	King and High Priest	Hebrews 7:1–28
7	A New Covenant	Hebrews 8:1–9:10
8	The Great Mediator	Hebrews 9:11–28
9	Faith, Hope, and Love	Hebrews 10:1–39
10	The Power of Faith	Hebrews 11:1–40
11	Running with Endurance	Hebrews 12:1–29
12	The Superior Life in Christ	Hebrews 13:1–25

SIX-WEEK FORMAT

Week	Lessons Covered	Reading
1	The Superiority of Christ / When God Became Man	Hebrews 1:1–2:18
2	A Soft Heart Toward God / Jesus Is All You Need	Hebrews 3:1–5:14
3	The Anchor of Hope / King and High Priest	Hebrews 6:1–7:28
4	A New Covenant / The Great Mediator	Hebrews 8:1–9:28
5	Faith, Hope, and Love / The Power of Faith	Hebrews 10:1–11:40
6	Running with Endurance / The Superior Life in Christ	Hebrews 12:1–13:25

In regard to organizing your time when planning your group Bible study, the following two schedules, for sixty minutes and ninety minutes, can give you a structure for the lesson:

Section	60 Minutes	90 Minutes
Welcome: Members arrive and get settled	5 minutes	10 minutes
Getting Started Question: Prepares the group for interacting with one another	10 minutes	10 minutes
Message: Review the lesson	15 minutes	25 minutes
Discussion: Discuss questions in the lesson	25 minutes	35 minutes
Review and Prayer: Review the key points of the lesson and have a closing time of prayer	5 minutes	10 minutes

As the group leader, it is up to you to keep track of the time and keep things moving according to your schedule. If your group is having a good discussion, don't feel the need to stop and move on to the next question. Remember, the purpose is to pull together ideas and share unique insights on the lesson. Encourage everyone to participate, but don't be concerned if certain group members are more quiet. They may just be internally reflecting on the questions and need time to process their ideas before they can share them.

Group Dynamics

Leading a group study can be a rewarding experience for you and your group members—but that doesn't mean there won't be challenges. Certain members may feel uncomfortable discussing topics that they consider very personal and might be afraid of being called on. Some members might have disagreements on specific issues. To help prevent these scenarios, consider the following ground rules:

- If someone has a question that may seem off topic, suggest that it be discussed at another time, or ask the group if they are okay with addressing that topic.

- If someone asks a question you don't know the answer to, confess that you don't know and move on. If you feel comfortable, invite other group members to give their opinions or share their comments based on personal experience.
- If you feel like a couple of people are talking much more than others, direct questions to people who may not have shared yet. You could even ask the more dominating members to help draw out the quiet ones.
- When there is a disagreement, encourage the group members to process the matter in love. Invite members from opposing sides to evaluate their opinions and consider the ideas of the other members. Lead the group through Scripture that addresses the topic, and look for common ground.

When issues arise, encourage your group to think of Scripture: "Love one another" (John 13:34), "If it is possible, as much as it depends on you, live peaceably with all men" (Romans 12:18), and, "Be swift to hear, slow to speak, slow to wrath" (James 1:19).

ABOUT
Dr. David Jeremiah and Turning Point

Dr. David Jeremiah is the founder of Turning Point, a ministry committed to providing Christians with sound Bible teaching relevant to today's changing times through radio and television broadcasts, audio series, books, and live events. Dr. Jeremiah's teaching on topics such as family, prayer, worship, angels, and biblical prophecy forms the foundation of Turning Point.

David and his wife, Donna, reside in El Cajon, California, where he serves as the senior pastor of Shadow Mountain Community Church. David and Donna have four children and twelve grandchildren.

In 1982, Dr. Jeremiah brought the same solid teaching to San Diego television that he shares weekly with his congregation. Shortly thereafter, Turning Point expanded its ministry to radio. Dr. Jeremiah's inspiring messages can now be heard worldwide on radio, television, and the internet.

Because Dr. Jeremiah desires to know his listening audience, he travels nationwide holding ministry rallies and spiritual enrichment conferences that touch the hearts and lives of many people. According to Dr. Jeremiah, "At some point in time, everyone reaches a turning point; and for every person, that moment is unique, an experience to hold onto forever. There's so much changing in today's world that sometimes it's difficult to choose the right path. Turning Point offers people an understanding of God's Word and seeks to make a difference in their lives."

Dr. Jeremiah has authored numerous books, including *Escape the Coming Night* (Revelation), *The Handwriting on the Wall* (Daniel), *Overcoming Loneliness*, *What in the World Is Going On?*, *The Coming Economic Armageddon*, *I Never Thought I'd See the Day!*, *God Loves You: He Always Has—He Always Will*, *Agents of the Apocalypse*, *Agents of Babylon*, *Revealing the Mysteries of Heaven*, *People Are Asking . . . Is This the End?*, *A Life Beyond Amazing*, *Overcomer*, *The Book of Signs*, *Everything You Need*, and *Forward*.

STAY CONNECTED
to Dr. David Jeremiah

Take advantage of two great ways to let Dr. David Jeremiah give you spiritual direction every day!

Turning Points Magazine and Devotional

Receive Dr. David Jeremiah's magazine, *Turning Points*, each month and discover:

- Thematic study focus
- 48 pages of life-changing reading
- Relevant articles
- Special features
- Daily devotional readings
- Bible study resource offers
- Live event schedule
- Radio & television information

Request *Turning Points* magazine today!
(800) 947-1993
www.DavidJeremiah.org/Magazine

Daily Turning Point E-Devotional

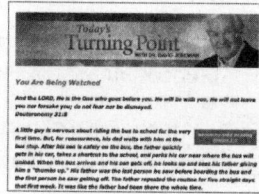

Start your day off right! Find words of inspiration and spiritual motivation waiting for you on your computer every morning! Receive a daily e-devotion communication from David Jeremiah that will strengthen your walk with God and encourage you to live the authentic Christian life.

Request your free e-devotional today!
(800) 947-1993
www.DavidJeremiah.org/Devo

New Bible Study Series from Dr. David Jeremiah

The Jeremiah Bible Study Series captures Dr. David Jeremiah's forty-plus years of commitment to teaching the whole Word of God. Each volume contains twelve lessons for individuals and groups to explore what the Bible says, what it meant to the people at the time it was written, and what it means to us today. Out of his lifelong ministry of *delivering the unchanging Word of God to an ever-changing world*, Dr. Jeremiah has written this Bible-strong study series focused not on causes, current events, or politics, but on the solid truth of Scripture.

9780310091493	Matthew	9780310091554	John	9780310091646	1 Corinthians
9780310091516	Mark	9780310091608	Acts	9780310097488	2 Corinthians
9780310091530	Luke	9780310091622	Romans	9780310091660	Galatians

Available now at your favorite bookstore.
More volumes coming soon.